The Abortion Controversy

Other Books in the Current Controversies Series:

The Abortion Controversy

Lynette Knapp, *Book Editor*

David Bender, *Publisher*
Bruno Leone, *Executive Editor*

Bonnie Szumski, *Editorial Director*
Stuart B. Miller, *Managing Editor*

CURRENT CONTROVERSIES

0084235

Cover photo: © Steve Starr/SABA

Library of Congress Cataloging-in-Publication Data

The abortion controversy / Lynette Knapp, book editor.—Rev. ed.
     p. cm. — (Current controversies)
  Includes bibliographical references and index.
  ISBN 0-7377-0333-4 (pbk. : alk. paper) — ISBN 0-7377-0334-2 (lib. bdg. : alk. paper)
   [1. Abortion.] I. Knapp, Lynette. II. Series.

HQ767 .A173   2001
363.46—dc21
                                   00-021331
                                      CIP

Contents

Chapter 1: Is Abortion Immoral?

Yes: Abortion Is Immoral

No: Abortion Is Not Immoral

numerous incidences of violence and murder prove that it is not a pro-life document.

Chapter 2: Should Abortion Rights Be Protected or Restricted?

Chapter 3: Should Women Have Greater Access to Abortion?

Chapter 4: Should Protesters Target Abortion Clinics and Providers?

No: Aborted Fetuses Should Not Be Used for Medical Research

Foreword

By definition, controversies are "discussions of questions in which opposing opinions clash" (Webster's Twentieth Century Dictionary Unabridged). Few would deny that controversies are a pervasive part of the human condition and exist on virtually every level of human enterprise. Controversies transpire between individuals and among groups, within nations and between nations. Controversies supply the grist necessary for progress by providing challenges and challengers to the status quo. They also create atmospheres where strife and warfare can flourish. A world without controversies would be a peaceful world; but it also would be, by and large, static and prosaic.

The Series' Purpose

The purpose of the Current Controversies series is to explore many of the social, political, and economic controversies dominating the national and international scenes today. Titles selected for inclusion in the series are highly focused and specific. For example, from the larger category of criminal justice, Current Controversies deals with specific topics such as police brutality, gun control, white collar crime, and others. The debates in Current Controversies also are presented in a useful, timeless fashion. Articles and book excerpts included in each title are selected if they contribute valuable, long-range ideas to the overall debate. And wherever possible, current information is enhanced with historical documents and other relevant materials. Thus, while individual titles are current in focus, every effort is made to ensure that they will not become quickly outdated. Books in the Current Controversies series will remain important resources for librarians, teachers, and students for many years.

In addition to keeping the titles focused and specific, great care is taken in the editorial format of each book in the series. Book introductions and chapter prefaces are offered to provide background material for readers. Chapters are organized around several key questions that are answered with diverse opinions representing all points on the political spectrum. Materials in each chapter include opinions in which authors clearly disagree as well as alternative opinions in which authors may agree on a broader issue but disagree on the possible solutions. In this way, the content of each volume in Current Controversies mirrors the mosaic of opinions encountered in society. Readers will quickly realize that there are many viable answers to these complex issues. By questioning each author's conclusions, students and casual readers can begin to develop the critical thinking skills so important to evaluating opinionated material.

Current Controversies is also ideal for controlled research. Each anthology in the series is composed of primary sources taken from a wide gamut of informational categories including periodicals, newspapers, books, United States and foreign government documents, and the publications of private and public organizations. Readers will find factual support for reports, debates, and research papers covering all areas of important issues. In addition, an annotated table of contents, an index, a book and periodical bibliography, and a list of organizations to contact are included in each book to expedite further research.

Perhaps more than ever before in history, people are confronted with diverse and contradictory information. During the Persian Gulf War, for example, the public was not only treated to minute-to-minute coverage of the war, it was also inundated with critiques of the coverage and countless analyses of the factors motivating U.S. involvement. Being able to sort through the plethora of opinions accompanying today's major issues, and to draw one's own conclusions, can be a complicated and frustrating struggle. It is the editors' hope that Current Controversies will help readers with this struggle.

Greenhaven Press anthologies primarily consist of previously published material taken from a variety of sources, including periodicals, books, scholarly journals, newspapers, government documents, and position papers from private and public organizations. These original sources are often edited for length and to ensure their accessibility for a young adult audience. The anthology editors also change the original titles of these works in order to clearly present the main thesis of each viewpoint and to explicitly indicate the opinion presented in the viewpoint. These alterations are made in consideration of both the reading and comprehension levels of a young adult audience. Every effort is made to ensure that Greenhaven Press accurately reflects the original intent of the authors included in this anthology.

Introduction

Much of the debate over abortion focuses on the issue of rights—specifically, whether a woman's right to an abortion outweighs a fetus's right to life. The two factions involved in this controversy are poles apart in their views on abortion: whereas the pro-choice movement contends that a woman's right to abortion is absolute, the pro-life movement asserts that a fetus's right to life is indisputable. Both sides rely on legal, scientific, and human rights arguments to support their arguments.

Behind this debate is the 1973 U.S. Supreme Court ruling in *Roe v. Wade,* which legalized abortion. *Roe* was based in part on the Fourteenth Amendment's right to privacy, which the Court ruled was "broad enough to encompass a woman's decision whether or not to terminate her pregnancy." According to the ruling, a woman's right to abortion outweighed the rights of a nonviable fetus and prohibited state interference. Even after viability, however, when the fetus could survive outside of the womb, the Court ruled that states must allow abortions that could save women's lives. In 1992 the Supreme Court reaffirmed *Roe* in *Planned Parenthood v. Casey,* maintaining a woman's fundamental right to abortion.

Abortion rights advocates have praised *Roe* and *Casey* for recognizing that a woman's right to control her body takes precedence over a fetus's right to life. These advocates stress that a woman's decision to control her reproduction is a private issue that does not concern the government. As the American Civil Liberties Union (ACLU) points out, "Enforcement of the idea that the fetus has legal rights superseding those of the woman who carries it would make pregnant women second-class citizens with fewer rights, and more obligations, than others." Just as it would be unthinkable to force someone to use their body to donate organs to preserve the life of a living person, the ACLU and other pro-choice organizations stress that it would be absurd to allow a fetus to use a woman's body as a life-support system without her consent.

Other members of the pro-choice movement emphasize that a woman's rights supercede those of a fetus, because the fetus is not yet a human being and therefore does not have the same rights as a woman. During pregnancy, they maintain, a fertilized ovum grows and develops, and eventually a separate, autonomous human being is born. Prior to birth, though, the fetus lacks the qualities of personhood—namely, sentience, social experience, and independent existence. The *Revolutionary Worker,* a publication of the Revolutionary Communist Party, explains: "[The fetus] is a developing mass of tissue integrally connected to the woman's vital biological processes. It is part of the woman with no separate social rights. For that it must have entered society as a separate entity. That is, it must have been born."

Feminists, along with abortion rights supporters, insist that a woman's right to privacy and bodily control must prevail over a fetus's right to life if women are to gain social and economic equality with men. In writing the plurality opinion in *Casey,* justices Sandra Day O'Connor, Anthony Kennedy, and David Souter support this belief: "The ability of women to participate equally in the economic and social life of the Nation has been facilitated in their ability to control their reproductive lives." Feminists argue that an unwanted pregnancy can often greatly hinder a woman's ability to finish school, remain working, or support herself financially. They stress that education and job rights are strongly protected by the Constitution, and in order to take advantage of these opportunities, women must be able to control their reproduction.

Members of the pro-life movement refute these arguments, however, arguing that *Roe* and *Casey* blatantly ignore the fetus's basic human rights. Critics of these rulings assert that the Fourteenth Amendment, which prohibits a state from depriving "any person of life, liberty, or property," does not give a woman the right to abort her fetus. Instead, they contend that the amendment protects all life and does not distinguish between living and unborn persons. According to the American Life League, "In addressing the argument that the preborn child is a 'person' deserving of protection under the Fourteenth Amendment's due-process clause . . . , the Court simply glosses over the scientific evidence of the preborn baby's humanity."

Abortion foes also argue that a woman's control over her body is not an absolute right. While a woman has power over her body and can choose how she would like to use it, laws can restrict her control when it infringes on the rights of others. As Frederica Mathewes-Green, an author, columnist for *Christianity Today,* and commentator for National Public Radio, states, "It is because I still believe so strongly in the right of a woman to protect her body that I now oppose abortion. That right must begin when her body begins, and it must be hers no matter where she lives—even if she lives in her mother's womb." Mathewes-Green believes that the right to control one's body can never eclipse the basic human rights of the fetus.

Most importantly, members of the pro-life movement contend that a fetus is indeed a separate, living human being whose rights begin in the womb and extend after birth. Supporters of a fetus's right to life point out that, although the fetus may lack the qualities that society associates with personhood, it is still a human life. Humanist and ethicist Diana Brown rejects the pro-choice claim that a fetus "is merely part of the mother's body and is entirely hers to dispose of. . . . Since the fetus is, however, genetically distinct from the mother, the latter position is hard to sustain." Others, like Brown, view life as a continuous process that begins at conception and continues until natural death.

Despite the longtime debate between members of the pro-choice and pro-life movements, the controversy over rights remains unresolved. Many abortion adversaries refuse to acknowledge the merits of their opponents' views, possibly fearing that any compromise might weaken their own position. Fervent pro-choicers reject all efforts to overturn *Roe* or restrict a woman's access to abortion. Likewise, impassioned pro-lifers object to abortion restrictions that protect some but not all fetuses. Whether a woman has an irrefutable right to abortion or whether a fetus has an unequivocal right to life are just two of the issues examined in *Abortion: Current Controversies*. While addressing the wide-ranging legal and moral aspects of the abortion controversy, this anthology also explores issues pertaining to abortion rights and accessibility, revolutionary abortifacients such as RU-486, contentious abortion procedures and research, and the escalating violence surrounding antiabortion protests.

Chapter 1

Is Abortion Immoral?

Chapter Preface

When the pro-life and pro-choice movements debate the morality of abortion, their arguments often center around the question of whether abortion is murder. Yet to resolve this controversy, both factions are faced with determining exactly when life begins—at fertilization, birth, or sometime in between. Members of the pro-life movement believe that abortion is murder because it intentionally kills a human being. As social services professor William Brennan explains, "When the abortionist invades the sanctuary of the womb, the passenger within is by all scientific criteria alive, growing, and developing. After the abortionist accomplishes his lethal task, the intrauterine victim is definitely no longer alive, and therefore dead. And it is the abortion procedure that brought about this death." The Catholic Church supports this belief, teaching that life begins at fertilization and any attempt to destroy that life—whether by abortion or contraception—is a sin. In 1995 Pope John Paul II officially condemned abortion in his "Evangelium Vitae," calling it a villainous crime that kills an innocent human being.

Members of the pro-choice movement contend, however, that abortion is a moral choice and therefore cannot be labeled as murder. Don Sloan, an obstetrician and gynecologist, agrees that while abortion destroys an embryo, it is only a potential human; an embryo lacks the brain activity, self-awareness, and social experience necessary for personhood. "I wouldn't deny that [embryos] are human tissue. Of course they are. . . . And while they're attached to the woman, that tissue is alive. But they're not independent life, and they're not people as we know them." Thus, abortion advocates assert, since an embryo or fetus is not viable or separate from its mother, its abortion is neither immoral nor murder.

When life begins and whether abortion is murder are two highly controversial issues in the abortion debate. In the following chapter, the authors examine these issues and others in an attempt to determine whether abortion is immoral.

Abortion Is Immoral

by Robert R. Reilly

About the author: *Robert R. Reilly is chairman of the Committee for Western Civilization.*

In *The Ethics* Aristotle wrote, "Men start revolutionary changes for reasons connected with their private lives." This is also true when revolutionary changes are cultural. What might these "private" reasons be, and why do they become public in the form of revolutionary changes? The answer to these questions lies in the intimate psychology of moral failure.

For any individual, moral failure is hard to live with because of the rebuke of conscience. Habitual moral failure, what used to be called vice, can be lived with only by obliterating conscience through rationalization. When we rationalize, we convince ourselves that heretofore forbidden desires are permissible. We advance the reality of the desires over the reality of the moral order to which the desires should be subordinated. In our minds we replace the reality of moral order with something more congenial to the activity we are excusing. In short, we assert that bad is good.

It is often difficult to detect rationalizations when one is living directly under their influence, and so historical examples are useful. One of the clearest was offered at the Nuremberg trials by Dr. Karl Brandt, who had been in charge of the Nazi regime's Aktion T-4 euthanasia program. He said in his defense: ". . . when I said 'yes' to euthanasia I did so with the deepest conviction, just as it is my conviction today, that it was right. Death can mean deliverance. Death is life."

The Power of Rationalization

Unlike Dr. Brandt, most people recover from their rationalizations when remorse and reality set back in. But when morally disordered acts become the defining centerpiece of one's life, vice can permanently pervert reason. Entrenched moral aberrations then impel people to rationalize vice not only to themselves but to others as well. Thus rationalizations become an engine for revolutionary change that will affect society as a whole.

The power of rationalization drives the culture war, gives it its particular revolutionary character, and makes its advocates indefatigable. It may draw its energy from desperation, but it is all the more powerful for that. Since failed rationalization means self-recrimination, it must be avoided at all cost. For this reason, the differences over which the culture war is being fought are not subject to reasoned discourse. Persons protecting themselves by rationalizing are interested not in finding the truth, but in maintaining the illusion that allows them to continue their behavior. For them to succeed in this, everyone must accede to their rationalization. This is why revolutionary change is required. The necessity for self-justification requires the complicity of the whole culture. Holdouts cannot be tolerated because they are potential rebukes. The self-hatred, anger, and guilt that a person possessed of a functioning conscience would normally feel from doing wrong are redirected by the rationalization and projected upon society as a whole (if the society is healthy), or upon those in society who do not accept the rationalization. . . .

The movement for abortion is . . . expansive in its claims upon society. The internal logic of abortion requires the spread of death from the unborn to the nearly born, and then to the infirm and otherwise burdensome individuals. The very psychology of rationalization also pushes those involved with abortion to spread the application of its principles in order to multiply the sources of support for it.

If you are going to kill innocent persons you had better convince yourself and others that it is "right," that you do it out of compassion. Thus, Beverly Harrison, a professor of Christian ethics at Union Theological Seminary, contends that abortion is a "positive good," and even a "loving choice." Jungian analyst Ginette

> *"When morally disordered acts become the defining centerpiece of one's life, vice can permanently pervert reason."*

Paris thinks it is even more. In her book, *The Sacrament of Abortion,* she calls for "new rituals as well as laws to restore to abortion its sacred dimension." Defending the right to partial-birth abortions during the 1996 U.S. Senate debate, Senator Barbara Boxer assured her colleagues that mothers who have aborted their children by this means "buried those babies with love." If abortion is love, then, indeed, as Dr. Brandt said, "Death is life."

Justifying Abortion

Abortion is the ultimate in the larger rationalization of the sexual revolution: if sex is only a form of amusement or self-realization (as it must be when divorced from the moral order), why should the generation of a child stand in the way of it, or penalize its fulfillment? The life of the child is a physical and moral rebuke to this proposition. But the child is too weak to overcome the power of the rationalization. The virtual reality of the rationalization is stronger than the actual reality of the child. The child succumbs to the rationalization and is killed in a new "sacrament."

With over 35 million abortions performed since 1973, the investment in the denial of the evil of abortion has become tremendous. Anyone who has witnessed the eruption of grief and horror (often coming many years after the event) in a woman confronting for the first time the nature of what she has done in an abortion knows the lengths to which people must go to prevent its occurrence.

> *"With over 35 million abortions performed since 1973, the investment in the denial of the evil of abortion has become tremendous."*

Thus the changing attitudes toward abortion can be directly traced to the growing number of people, including fathers, doctors, and nurses, with the need to justify it. As reported by the Kaiser Family Foundation, the number of people who think abortion should be illegal in all circumstances has declined from 21 per cent in 1975 to only 15 per cent in 1995. The proportion who support abortion in all circumstances has increased from 21 per cent to 33 per cent in the same period. This change has taken place not because pro-abortionists are winning arguments, but because of the enormous increase in the number of those with a personal, psychological need to deny what abortion is.

Controversies about life, generation, and death are decisive for the fate of any civilization. A society can withstand any number of persons who try to advance their own moral disorders as public policy. But it cannot survive once it adopts the justifications for those moral disorders as its own.

Selective Abortion Is Immoral

by Lori Brannigan Kelly

About the author: *Lori Brannigan Kelly, a former White House staff member during the Reagan administration, is a freelance writer.*

So far as I know, this century's first "cost-based" proposal for the selective killing of "worthless" humans appeared in a monograph published in Leipzig, Germany, in 1920—more than a dozen years before Adolf Hitler came to power. In an essay entitled *Permitting the Destruction of Unworthy Life,* Dr. Karl Binding wrote:

> Since they require extensive care, they occasion the development of a profession devoted to providing years and decades of care for absolutely valueless lives. . . . Again, I find no grounds, legally, socially, ethically or religiously— for not permitting the killing of these people, who are the fearsome counter image of true humanity.

On June 1, 1995, Domenica Lawson was born in England with Down's syndrome. The fact that Domenica was born at all is significant, because, on both sides of the Atlantic, the 75-year-old brainchild of Dr. Binding is also alive and well. Indeed, it is being applied to "valueless" lives at the earliest possible point—in utero. A special prenatal-screening process is now widely available to expectant parents; it can detect many if not all genetic abnormalities in the fetus during the first few months of pregnancy. If such abnormalities are found, it is now "normal" for the would-have-been parents to have the defective fetus aborted. Needless to add, such "selective" abortions, including those based solely on the baby's gender, are perfectly legal in both the U.S. and Britain.

Reaction to Domenica's Birth

Little Domenica beat the odds; she was not aborted. But her birth ignited an often-bitter debate on the high cost of "unworthy" life. Her father is Dominic Lawson, a professed atheist who was then the editor of the *Spectator,* a highly-

Excerpted from Lori Brannigan Kelly, "The Faustian Cost of Prenatal Testing," *Human Life Review*, Winter 1996. Reprinted with permission from the author.

respected weekly opinion journal. . . . He wrote an article celebrating Domenica's arrival and his abhorrence of the British health system's policy of providing "gratis, an abortion, if their tests show that the mother is expecting a Down's baby."

Lawson's story caused a great deal of comment, and many letters, some of which were printed in the *Spectator.* One, from a woman with severe spina bifida, thanked Lawson, adding ". . . occasionally there are reports of doctors who starve to death born babies with my degree of disability because they think we are 'better off dead' . . . in recognising [Domenica's] infinite value and worth you also recognised mine." A parent of a 23-year-old Down's man wrote poignantly of ". . . this extraordinary syndrome which deletes anger and malice, replacing them with humour, thoughtfulness and devotion to friend and family." She lovingly described her son, and others like him, as "stars in an increasingly materialistic world."

But praise was by no means all Lawson got back. In a column headlined "A Duty to Choose Unselfishly" Claire Rayner of the *Independent* castigated the Lawsons for refusing prenatal tests—the burden of their decision and the "misery" of Domenica's life would now have to be shared by society. The Lawsons, wrote Rayner, would ultimately not be "paying the full price of their choice."

Cost-Effectiveness and Human Life

Rayner's gratuitous indignation is typical of the "climate of cost-effectiveness" that surrounds the use of prenatal testing. Ostensibly, testing is intended to relieve parental fears about the viability and well-being of their unborn child, and to provide them—and their doctors—with advance information that could be of vital importance. But in practice such information is being used to pressure parents into the "choice" of abortion. Thus, if a fetus is found to be of poor biological or genetic quality, the infant itself is increasingly looked upon as having a negative economic and social net worth, since the estimated costs of its sustained care over the course of a lifetime are obviously far greater than the costs of aborting it. For screening programs to be cost-effective and useful for the entire population, proponents like Rayner argue, couples must use the information they receive to avoid—through abortion—the birth of a genetically diseased infant.

> *"What price do we pay when our focus on balancing the bottom line virtually ignores the sanctity of human life?"*

As prenatal technology increasingly makes possible a cost-efficient "thinning of the ranks," what will the future hold for children with congenital abnormalities? What impact will the pre-birth elimination of such individuals have on society? And, most importantly, what price do we pay when our focus on balancing the bottom line virtually ignores the sanctity of human life itself? Here in the U.S., where annual health-care costs now exceed 14% of the gross domestic product, the continuing debate is focused on ways and means to at least cut the steady growth of medical expenses. There is mounting pressure to ration treatment (it is already happening in Oregon) by cost-benefit analyses; in short, to spend our shrinking resources only on the curable. In such a strictly-utilitarian economy, unborn babies judged to be incurable are easy targets.

Cost-benefit analysis is one thing when used for making decisions about the allocations of scarce or limited resources, but quite another when divorced from moral or political guidance and direction. It is true that, in today's economically-oriented

> *"Insurance companies . . . are playing an increasing role in coercing families to terminate 'problem' pregnancies."*

society, cost-benefit analysis is inevitable. In the area of prenatal research, however, what remains to be seen is just what kind of principles will guide its use. Patrick Derr, a professor of philosophy at Clark University, has convincingly argued that cost-benefit analysis should in no instance be a morally-neutral enterprise. When cost is separated from ethics, Derr says, the moral foundations of a society are undermined, leading to a radical individualism and nihilism that can ultimately jeopardize the common life of our democracy. A theory of medicine that is predicated on a merely utilitarian vision of life will self-destruct. According to Derr, what is sometimes seen in neonatal applications is that the "technicians involved are doing calculations with value judgments that society and law would reject. Their science may be good, but what's wrong is that before attempting their science, they're foisting [upon society] value judgments that are not universally held.". . .

Fear, Coercion, and Exploitation

But what actually compels women to test and, subsequently, to have abortions in these cases? In one illuminating *New York Times* Op-Ed piece, Dr. Kenneth Prager, associate clinical professor of medicine at Columbia College of Physicians and Surgeons, blames the proliferation of prenatal testing on a kind of individualistic hedonism. In the United States, he writes, patients commonly "believe they have an unlimited right to the most expensive care, no matter how inappropriate the circumstances, and . . . wish to have their fears of illness allayed, no matter how remote its likelihood." Expectant parents commonly fear the unknown. Prenatal technology can provide them with an abundance of information about their unborn child, but the science is admittedly imperfect and expensive. Some parents demand testing despite its cost and, should there be a problem with the accuracy of the prenatal report, there is now legal recourse. So-called "wrongful life" lawsuits, in which parents sue their physicians for withholding results of a genetic test, or for providing inaccurate reports that "resulted" in the unwanted birth, are increasing dramatically.

The fear of such malpractice claims actually propels the prenatal testing machine forward. For "Pro-choice" testing advocates, as well as litigation-wary physicians, the more parents know and the earlier they know it, the less the risk of a "costly" child being born. And there are other participants in this "industry" that have a vested interest in the in vitro guarantee of human physical perfection: without question, insurance companies—and insurance economics—are playing an increasing role in coercing families to terminate "problem" pregnancies. There are already reports of cases in which insurance carriers have attempted to deny coverage when prenatal abnormalities are detected. Dr. Robert Fink, a pulmonary specialist who treats cystic fibrosis patients at the Children's National Medical Center in Washington, D.C., calls this "prenatal blackmail.". . .

Dr. Fink claims that one expectant Catholic couple in suburban Maryland, who already had a child with cystic fibrosis, were told by their health maintenance organization that their policy would pay for prenatal testing, but only if the couple agreed to abort if the test detected another fetus with cystic fibrosis. In a clearly-coercive move, the HMO implied that if the parents decided to bring an abnormal pregnancy to term, the infant would be denied benefits altogether. Says Fink: "It's illegal to cancel group policies, but not illegal to raise rates [to force families out of care]. What we have seen locally is that the insurance companies are typically represented by individual case managers who push intimidation, but know they will ultimately lose in court.". . .

> *"Behind every ultrasound, amniocentesis and blood-sample test there is the real flesh, blood and bone of a child."*

Exactly what effect does the expansion of scientific research have on the growing exploitation of prenatal testing? One biotechnology insider, interviewed on the basis of anonymity, has this to say: "For most researchers, the general goal of prenatal genetic science is the understanding and prevention of illness on a genetic level, not the termination of unwanted, abnormal children." She also argues that cost-benefit analysis has always been an implicit factor in research, but that its presence has neither driven nor tainted the nobler aim of science. But is this always true? In the last decade, both in medical literature and in scientific laboratories, cost-benefit analysis has come to the forefront, and there can be little doubt, given all the financial calculations currently applied to testing, that many researchers see prenatal screening's main function to be the targeting and elimination of "unwanted" and/or "abnormal" life—surely an alarming trend. . . .

In short, . . ."cost-benefit" proposals for aggressive testing—aimed directly at the termination of prenatal life—demonstrate what happens when science is detached from morality. They also raise the question: Where are the millions needed to fund such "research" coming from? And, if much of it is U.S. government money, does it not put our government's imprimatur on the "results"—

including lethal policies that many if not most taxpayers might strongly oppose? The reality is that, despite all the talk of "cost-effectiveness," huge amounts of federal and private money are being spent on "prenatal screening" that targets defective infants. In 1995, the National Institute of Child Health and Human Development (NICH) contributed over $7 million to projects concerned with prenatal diagnosis. Over $5 million went to the development of a perinatal research facility at Georgetown University, a Jesuit institution. A closer look at other NICH grants is also enlightening. The foundation for Blood Research in Scarborough, Maine, was awarded $368,502 for a project which involved a "feasibility analysis" to determine whether introducing "screening measurements for Down's syndrome can be justified in the first trimester, based on cost and medical efficacy.". . .

Valuing the Imperfect

As the pressure to kill the imperfect among us increases, and as a cost-benefit analysis of prenatal research divorced from any recognition of the sanctity of human life continues to grow in acceptance, the argument must time and again be made that, behind every ultrasound, amniocentesis and blood-sample test there is the real flesh, blood and bone of a child. A child who will someday celebrate, glorify, revere and reflect the eternal. Who among us can say that their lives, in whatever form they may take, will not somehow deliver back to us what is best in us?

We will not know their worth unless we hold them tenderly in our hands, regard the mystery of their afflicted shape, and . . . translate their shape into symbol, their symbol into words, and those words into commonly accepted truths about the benevolence of creation. For society to be able to do this, it must possess a language that is circumscribed by faith and rooted in the civic ethos of a principled democracy, one that respects all human life, accepts the unavoidable nature of suffering, and recognizes the existence of a moral authority outside—and beyond—itself.

It is not unlikely that, in just a matter of years, first-trimester prenatal screening using maternal blood samples could be perfected to detect the unborn asthmatic, the mentally ill, the diabetic, the autistic, and the dyslexic. What will come of these test results? Where will the gods of cost-efficiency lead us then? Who will defend the multitude of flawed lives that may be deemed too economically burdensome to exist?

Ultimately, we must ask ourselves: How many marked generations will, without vigilance, be silently thrown out to sea?

Abortion Is Murder

by Michael McKenzie

About the author: *Michael McKenzie is an adjunct professor of religion and philosophy at Northwest College.*

Nobody ever called General George S. Patton squeamish. In his memoirs of World War II, as he fought his way across France and Germany, Patton describes destroyed German tanks, bombed-out buildings, and even hideously burned German corpses with a martial relish. To him, that was a normal part of war. But all this death and destruction which was a part of Patton's world paled next to his first encounter with what were called "horror camps" or "hell camps."

In fact, the horrors of the Ohrdruf camp even caused the hardened Patton to become physically sick and to label it "the most appalling sight imaginable." The evils were so incredible, and disproved so thoroughly the notion that reported Nazi evils were mere propaganda, that Patton conceived of the idea of having first American soldiers and newsmen, then the local German inhabitants come view the camps themselves.

From the very first contacts between the German civilian populace and the horrors of the camps, it was clear that some seemed to know very little about what was going on there, most had a pretty good idea, and still others aided and abetted their Nazi masters. Patton himself believed that most of the local civilians were ignorant of the "infamies" which occurred at Ohrdruf, and instead placed much of the blame on the local *Gauleiter,* a minor Nazi functionary who was responsible for party control in that area.

From early on, however, there was also a healthy dose of skepticism regarding the supposed ignorance of the civilians who lived near the death camps. After all, didn't they ever notice the arriving cattle trains packed with their horrible human cargo? Weren't they suspicious when the wind blew the wrong way and the unmistakable odor of burning flesh assailed their nostrils? Were there ever no instances such as the unforgettable scene in the movie *Schindler's List,* when ash from a nearby crematorium blanketed a local town? How about the stories of various escapees and survivors? Were they given no credence whatsoever? Certainly such thoughts must have been in the back of the reporter's mind who asked Lieutenant General Walter Bedell Smith at a press conference in 1945, "And they [the local citizenry] say they didn't know about it [the horrors of the camps]?"

Frankly, the just verdict of history has been pronounced upon the German *volk* who either claimed ignorance, fear, or impotence as a reason for not acting against the Nazi Reich. After all, some brave Germans *did* act. Many of the "Confessing German Church" paid a heavy price for their opposition; some indeed paid the ultimate price. Thus, the German civilians do indeed bear their own moral responsibility for what went on at the death camps. There is culpability in helping to bring Hitler to power; there certainly is culpability in support of the Nazi war effort; and there is culpability in the self-induced mass blindness to what was happening to the Jews. No respect for authority, no claims of ignorance, and no protestations of powerlessness do anything to remove the stigma which has settled over the German civilians of that period. Even silent opposition on their part was not enough. When barbarous evil is going on, those present have a moral duty to speak out, even to act.

Christians as Idle Spectators

As I studied the history of World War II, I must admit to feeling no little anger—and a little smugness—toward those same Germans who claimed ignorance in the face of such barbarous evil. I comforted myself with the thought that such hypocrisy and cowardice could never happen here in America. Then, as I began to study the abortion issue in depth, a number of disquieting propositions took shape in my mind. They came in no particular order; in fact I had believed most of them for a long time. However, I had never before put them all together. These propositions were: 1) fully human life begins at conception; 2) in America alone, abortion was therefore killing about 2 million *people* every year; 3) there were a lot of Christians in this country who believed that both the above propositions were absolutely true; 4) the vast majority of those Christians—including myself—didn't act like we believed it; 5) thus, the American church is morally analogous to those Germans half a century ago who protested that they either: didn't know, didn't care, or couldn't act.

Hence I found myself in the position of a German *Bürgermeister*, lacking only the final forced inspection of the camps. What were my ex-

> **"When barbarous evil is going on, those present have a moral duty to speak out, even to act."**

cuses for my own inaction? Did not the very same reasons which so justly condemned the German civilians also condemn me? Was I not a culpable spectator at a devilish circus far worse than any envisioned half a century ago? Granted, there are differences, even important ones, between the abortion tragedy and the Holocaust. But if one believes that life, real life with all the attendant moral cords and claims of personhood, begins at conception, then are there any *moral* differences in the killing? Thus, those of us who believe that abortion snuffs out the life of a human *person* have some unpleasant comparisons to face.

A number of proposed explanations of the dilemma never made much headway in my thought. Some Christians explained their inaction by stating obvious governmental differences between the Nazi regime and ours; others made the point that abortion is legal here, and the Nazi horrors came at the expense of even their own laws; still others pointed out that the Holocaust itself occurred during time of war, and is therefore disanalogous to

> *"Those of us who believe that abortion snuffs out the life of a human* **person** *have some unpleasant comparisons to face."*

today. Some writers focused on the entire issue of voluntarism: after all, elective abortion is not compulsory abortion. A few thinkers attempted to distinguish between human life and human personhood, believing the latter category to be of more moral worth than the former. One last answer even concerned itself with the *destiny* of the aborted baby. That is, unlike the situation with the Jewish Holocaust, at least we could comfort ourselves with the fact that the aborted unborn are in heaven.

I found all of these explanations not only philosophically and theologically unsatisfying but really beside the point. For one thing, none of them really deal with the heart of the matter: whether or not Christians are acting as idle spectators in the presence of mass murder. For another, many of the writers seemed quite ready to defend their own inaction, while admitting that an actual genocide was taking place. . . .

It is my thesis that the unborn in this country are suffering a persecution which follows the same basic sociological patterns as other persecutions; and the only way to mitigate the persecution is to attack the patterns at their own key presuppositions.

The Patterns of Persecution

In a helpful work, R.I. Moore identifies the main stages in the development of a persecuting society. . . .

The first step necessary for a group to be targeted for persecution is the obvious but no less essential requirement that the group be capable of ready identification. Moore calls this process "classification," and whether it is due to clothing, location, appearance, language, or habits, the "enemy to society" must first be able to be identified as a group, so as not to be perceived primarily as individuals. It is interesting to our study to make the point that such ready identification sometimes came from earlier good motives. For example, Moore points out that society had often set Jewish communities apart in order to "protect their religious and cultural identity." Tragically, this "identification for protection" was later turned against the Jews when the political and social climates changed. When writing about the Armenian genocide at the hands of the Turks, Donald E. Miller and Lorna T. Miller comment that this step necessitates that the victim group be "perceived to fall short of being fully human. It is only when the victim group is dehumanized through such labeling that genocide can occur."

The second stage concerns the development of a socially constructed myth which labels the identified group as a source of social contamination and danger. A key component of this stage is the recognition that this myth may be founded "upon whatever foundation of reality." The notable feature is not whether the myth is true, but whether it can serve to collectively energize and mobilize the populace to recognize the danger posed by the group in question.

Thus, such myths are often composed in apocalyptic language: "the threat which the victims present is omnipresent, and so highly contagious as to be virtually irresistible. . . . [T]his is the language of fear, and of the fear of social change. Moore sums it up by saying that "pollution fear, in other words, is the fear that the privileged feel of those at whose expense their privilege is enjoyed." We can see this scapegoat language exemplified in how the Nazis held the Jews responsible during World War II for treason, treachery, weakness of the German allies, disease, greed, and weakness of German morale. In fact, for Joseph Goebbels, head of the Nazi propaganda machine, the entire war could be summed up as the "life-and-death struggle between the Aryan race and the Jewish bacillus."

Clearly, the use of dehumanizing language serves as a dialectic transition between classification and myth-making. When Goebbels employed the term "bacillus," it was meant not only to classify the Jews, but also to portray them as less than human agents of fear in the Nazi myth of racial superiority. Thus, language can act as both cause and effect within the sociological forces which propel persecution. Its use is both an attempt to force people to see others in a new light and the result of new and different attitudes and presuppositions. . . .

Lastly, genocide is often carried out "in conditions that discourage intervention by outside parties." This is done as a tacit acknowledgment that if people *really knew* what was going on "behind those walls," they may not approve and hence attempt to intervene. This is also, of course, an acknowledgment by the persecutors that there is a universal moral sense and that their acts are violating that sense. Having discussed the social categories which shape (and are shaped by) persecution and genocide in general, let us now examine how abortion fits the historical patterns.

> *"The unborn in this country are suffering a persecution which follows the same basic sociological patterns as other persecutions."*

The unborn constitute one of the most easily definable groups possible. They are dependent on another easily definable population (i.e., women) for their very survival, they make their presence known by unmistakable signs during pregnancy, they are never confused with other groups, and they are not readily thought of as individuals. The latter characteristic will quite rightly be questioned by those people who have developed strong feelings of affection for the individual unborn child. But such feelings are usually limited to those with ties to the mother or the family. My point here is only that a disinterested observer of a pregnant woman is likely to relate her (and her unborn child) to others of the same class and type, rather than thinking in terms of the unborn child and mother as consisting of two separate individuals. Ironically, as was the case with the Jews historically, such separation of the unborn was once made almost wholly for positive reasons. Recognizing the fact that pregnancy was almost universally admired and desired in this country, our entire society went out of its way to cater to the expectant mother and her unborn baby. Although it would be far from the truth to suggest that all such feelings have vanished, it is not claiming too much to notice that neither the universality nor the level of societal approval of pregnancy has maintained the level of the past. The reason for that downswing brings us to the second requirement for persecution.

> *"Genocide is often carried out 'in conditions that discourage intervention by outside parties.'"*

The Overpopulation Myth

It used to be that it was mainly Christians themselves who claimed that the world was about to end. This is no more the case. To see current apocalyptic works . . . one travels not to the Christian bookstore, but to the environmental section of the local library. Here those with advanced degrees in the sciences have taken the mantle of secular prophets, warning their readers that their very existence—*earth's* very existence—is threatened with nearly inevitable doom. Of course the causes of this peril are typically legion: toxic waste, air pollution, water pollution, ozone depletion, and destruction of the rain forest all vie in a showcase seemingly designed to scare us half to death. But the one crisis which always seems to lead the list, the "mother of all catastrophes" (pun intended), is the claim that overpopulation will soon lead to irreversible calamity. In fact, it is claimed that overpopulation is actually the *cause* of all the other disasters.

Unquestionably, the guru of this apocalyptic thought is biologist Paul Ehrlich of Stanford University. . . . Ehrlich claims that the "population problem" is our number one environmental crisis, that it is inevitably linked to all other environmental crises we face today, and that unless it is solved, it is in fact pointless to try and solve any other threats to the environment. We must act now to limit births, he states; else nature will step in and do the same thing by global starvation. . . .

It is not just the overpopulation myth which paints pregnancy and the unborn as scapegoats. That is, when a woman becomes pregnant in this sort of social climate, she is more and more aware of the popular spin on population issues. If she decides to keep the baby, she obviously has decided to weather these forces, basically making her and her unborn child part of the same "team." If this truly represents a case of "you and me against the world," there are other sociological forces which attempt to pry between the unborn child and the mother, painting the unborn as a threat, not against the world at large, but against the mother herself.

Autonomy, Freedom, and Rhetoric

These arguments originate mainly from radical feminism, with the woman's autonomy and freedom the main issues at stake. With the concept of "choice" so all-important now, it can be forgiven someone if he or she thinks that just the concept of choice itself is more important than the option chosen. It is in this vein that Judith Jarvis Thomson gives us her famous analogy of the unconscious violinist. She asks us to believe that pregnancy is analogous to a person being hooked up involuntarily to a violinist, their kidneys being needed to cleanse the musician's circulatory system. Thomson gives us this portrait to attempt to show us that even if the unborn is admitted to be fully human (as is the violinist), that doesn't mean that the mother (the one with the healthy kidneys) must keep him or her alive. Thus, the unborn child is now perceived as a threat against the mother's right to choose, her right to be independent. . . .

It is important to reiterate that this threat to the mother posed by the unborn has nothing to do with physical endangerment. It is instead framed as if the unborn is solely a threat to the mother's total autonomy, her desired way of life. Ironically, I see these arguments as themselves acting in powerful and pervasive ways upon modern women, actually influencing them *from without* in much the same way as many feminists accuse the "patriarchally dominated society" of doing. Thus, true autonomy is a fiction; the real issue is an evaluation of the ideas which constantly compete to influence us.

Hence, the killing of the unborn clearly meets the two criteria of classification and scapegoat myth. The apocalyptic language is stronger in the formulation of the overpopulation myth, but it is not uncommon for "pro-choice" rhetoric to bring in similar language of fear. It is the fear of rights being taken away, the seemingly countless women killed by "back-alley abortions"; it is the fear of American women regressing into the primitive and patriarchal past. This common language of fear, and the realization that the same group is the scapegoat in both myths, convinces me that these two myths—the unborn as threat to *both* world and mother—are really two sides of the same coin. Hence, these two myths coalesce to form a doubly heavy weight: women are pressured to abort to save the world, *and* to preserve their "happiness and freedom." If one is convinced that

> *"Sociological forces . . . attempt to pry between the unborn child and the mother, painting the unborn as a threat."*

his or her action is both morally praiseworthy *and* conducive to personal happiness, that is a powerful influence indeed. Bystanders feel these pressures no less keenly. Men are especially hesitant to speak out against abortion, fearing that they will be charged with oppressing women. . . .

Societal Pressures

It is often said by pro-lifers that if there was a window into the womb, there would be fewer abortions. Probably so. Quite rightly, if we could see the miracle of life unfolding, there would no doubt be less desire to destroy it. But more to the point, if abortions were performed in a more accessible setting, or if attendance at an abortion were somehow made mandatory for all of society, there would doubtlessly be fewer abortions still. As it is, however, abortions are performed in places that are walled off from the public; and 2 million unborn are killed each year in this country in complete anonymity. Some of the insulation is obviously due to the abortion centers becoming focal points of violence. Nevertheless, it is valid to ask whether abortion would be as popular if all of us could see what the abortionist sees. Certainly, it cannot be questioned that abortion, like the historical examples of genocide, deliberately takes place as far away from the public eye as possible.

Thus, abortion as the persecution—even genocide—of the unborn fits the social pattern of other persecutions and genocides. The pressures brought to bear by abortion advocates are framed in much the same way as was

> *"Women are pressured to abort to save the world, and to preserve their 'happiness and freedom.'"*

the case with other dominant, persecuting groups: the victim group is identified and classified, and then typecast as villain and scapegoat in a foundational myth. To oppose this myth is to oppose the greater good (either world survival or the mother's autonomy). The unborn as scapegoat is fully realized in our troubled times of moral relativism; and abortion becomes our "dirty little secret," hidden away from public scrutiny. . . .

These pressures not only undoubtedly influence prospective mothers, but also society at large. For example, 50 percent of those claiming to be "Born-Again Christians" label environmentalism a "very important issue" which influences their voting patterns. Also, the birthrate has fallen steadily in the United States and is now at approximately 1.8 children per couple. Clearly, at some level, we in this country have bought into the idea that there are entirely too many people in the world and we should do our part to correct that problem. . . .

Toward the Future

In view of how these social pressures are formed, and how they act to influence all those involved in the abortion issue, we Christians must act to reverse their pervasive effects. First, we must strive to "re-humanize" the unborn.

Whether by pointing to the strides made by fetology in showing us the remarkable abilities of the unborn, or by our own use of nonsterile language, we must insist on utilizing every device possible which stresses the humanity of nascent life. This linkage between the born and the unborn serves to reduce the tendency to see the unborn as a special group, ready for classification and persecution.

Second, we must attack the foundational myth at its source. Despite the politically correct views of the day, scientists themselves are sharply divided on whether or not a population crisis even exists. There are excellent data which suggest that the entire idea of an apocalyptic overpopulation crisis is a gross simplification of a complex issue, and a rehashing of outdated and misguided theories. Christians should make themselves aware of such data and dispute the doomsayers, effectively cutting the connection between the myth and the unborn.

> **"We must strive to 're-humanize' the unborn."**

Third, the idea that pregnancy is a gift from God and something to be cherished ought to be encouraged. Understanding the inevitable links between societal attitudes and laws, it is nevertheless the case that pregnant women should get special considerations, concerning everything from more convenient parking spaces to better seats on buses. Relatedly, Christians should lobby against laws which discourage pregnancy (i.e., by taxation).

Fourth, keeping in mind the Miller's point that genocide often thrives in secrecy, Christians ought to continue exposing what goes on in abortion clinics. Whether or not abortion is "America's dirty little secret," many Christians (and others of good-will) would be horrified to see an actual abortion. Questions of taste must pale before issues of genocide—we have a responsibility to show the truth. Historically, public exposure has tended to discourage genocide; perhaps abortion will follow this pattern. I must admit, however, that I am not overly optimistic.

As I write this, the avenues open for Christians to actively protest abortion are being slowly, yet inexorably, choked. Legislative attempts by various states to restrict or modify *Roe v. Wade* have generally been overturned. As mentioned, draconian fines and prison terms have often been levied against those who dare even to *peacefully* protest at clinic locations. Socially, protesters are pariahs, cast as fanatics on the extreme fringes of society.

Within the Christian community itself, there are signs that apathy toward abortion is growing, tending to polarize evangelicals even further. Many Christians are simply tired of it all. "We tried our best, our efforts failed, it's all in God's hands now." This closure of what have always been viewed in America as legitimate avenues of protest will undoubtedly serve to energize those who see even civil disobedience as not going far enough. Violence at abortion clinics and violence against abortionists will be sporadic but will not go away. To quote Dickens's Ghost of Christmas Present, "if these shadows remain unaltered by the Future," the persecution, the genocide of the unborn will continue; and we Christians will pray, write many books and letters of protest, and continue life very much as before. But let us not do one thing: let us not point with accusing fingers at the busy German people of half a century ago and shrilly denounce them for idly sitting by while 6 million Jews went to their deaths. Instead, let us pray for strength and wisdom, asking the Lord what exactly He would have us do, and then let us quietly ask for mercy and forgiveness.

Abortion Is a Moral Choice

by Henry Morgentaler

About the author: *Henry Morgentaler is a longtime advocate of abortion rights. He opened Canada's first abortion clinic in 1968 and was tried four times on charges of providing illegal abortions. His 1973 acquittal by a jury was overturned by the Court of Appeal of Quebec and upheld by the Supreme Court of Canada. Canada's House of Commons subsequently passed the Morgentaler Amendment, making it unconstitutional to overturn a jury acquittal. Morgentaler is also the author of* Abortion and Contraception.

This is a very appropriate time for me to write on "The Moral Case for Abortion." Many people in the pro-choice community believe that the battle for reproductive freedom has been won, that abortion is now available, that women have gained control over their reproductive capacities and have been liberated from the repressive rulings of patriarchal governments. This is not completely true.

There are still many countries in the world where women are subjected to the dogmatic religious edicts of theocracies. There are still women willing to endanger their health, future fertility, and even their lives in order to terminate an unwanted pregnancy. The religious right and the anti-abortion movement is gaining ground on this continent and abroad. Even here, in the United States, where everyone hoped that *Roe v. Wade* would forever ensure a woman's right to choice, the violent factions of the anti-abortion movement are waging war on doctors, staff, and abortion clinics; and political lobby groups and presidential candidates violently opposed to choice are within reach of the Oval Office. There are even members of the pro-choice community who are questioning the morality of reproductive freedom. These people believe that abortion must be available, but that it is inherently bad—a necessary evil. This attitude is dangerous and destructive and undermines the enormous gains due to the availability of good abortion services. In fact, the decision to have an abortion is clearly an extremely moral choice; it is a choice that liberates, empowers, and benefits women and society. In this viewpoint, I will examine all these issues from a humanist perspective, and reaffirm the morality of reproductive choice.

Excerpted from Henry Morgentaler, "The Moral Case for Abortion," *Free Inquiry*, Summer 1996. Reprinted with permission from *Free Inquiry*.

Humanist Ethics vs. Religious Attitudes

The issue of the morality of abortion provides the best illustration of the profound difference between humanist ethics and traditional religious attitudes. The former are based on concern for individual and collective well-being and are able to incorporate all available modern data and knowledge; whereas the latter are bound by dogma and tradition to sexist, irrational prohibitions against abortion and women's rights and are completely and callously indifferent to the enormous, avoidable suffering such attitudes are inflicting on individuals and on the community.

Most of the debate raging about abortion around the world has centered around the question of morality. Is it ever moral or responsible for a woman to request and receive an abortion, or is abortion always immoral, sinful, and criminal?

When you listen to the rhetoric of the anti-abortion faction, or read imprecise terms about the unborn, you get the impression that every abortion kills a child; consequently it cannot be condoned under any circumstances, with the sole exception of when the life of the pregnant woman is endangered by the pregnancy, a condition that is now extremely rare. This position—that abortion is always wrong and that there is a human being in the womb from the moment of conception—is a religious idea mostly propagated by the doctrine of the Roman Catholic church and espoused by many fundamentalist Protestant groups, though not by the majority of Catholics and Protestants.

> *"The decision to have an abortion is . . . a choice that liberates, empowers, and benefits women and society."*

Let us briefly examine this idea. At the moment of conception the sperm and the ovum unite, creating one cell. To proclaim that this one cell is already a full human being and should be treated as such is so patently absurd that it is almost difficult to refute. It is as if someone claimed that one brick is already a house and should be treated with the same respect a full house deserves. Even if you have a hundred bricks, or two hundred bricks, it is not yet a house. For it to be a house it needs walls, plumbing, electricity, and a functional organization. The same is true for a developing embryo. In order for it to be a human being it needs an internal organization, organs, and especially a human brain to be considered fully human. This entity is the result of sexual intercourse, where procreation is often not the goal, and whether it is called a zygote, blastocyst, embryo, or fetus, it does not have all the attributes of a human being and thus cannot properly be considered one.

If abortion is always viewed as "intentional murder," why isn't miscarriage viewed in similar terms? After all, almost half of all embryos are spontaneously shed in what is called "miscarriage" or "spontaneous abortion." If spontaneous abortions are an "act of God," to use the common religious expression, is it not strange that God has so little concern for fetal life that He allows so much of it to go to waste without intervening? Is it not possible to then conclude that God does not mind or object to spontaneous abortions? Why is it that the Catholic church has no ritual to mark the abortion of so much fetal life when it occurs spontaneously, yet becomes so vociferous and condemnatory when it is a conscious decision by a woman or couple?

Abortion Considers the Potential Life

I believe that an early embryo may be called a potential human being. But remember that every woman has the potential to create twenty-five human beings in her lifetime. The idea that any woman who becomes pregnant as a result of non-procreative sexual intercourse must continue with her pregnancy does not take into consideration the fact that there is a tremendous discrepancy between the enormous potential of human fertility and the real-life ability of women and couples to provide all that is necessary to bring up children properly. The morality of any act cannot be divorced from the foreseeable consequences of that act. Should a girl of twelve or a woman of forty-five, or any woman for that matter, be forced to continue a pregnancy or be saddled with bringing up a child for eighteen years without any regard for the consequences, without any regard for the expressed will or desire of that woman, or of the couple? . . .

Haven't we learned anything by observing events in countries where abortion is illegal, where women are forced to abort fetuses themselves or by the hands of quacks, where many die and more are injured for life or lose their fertility? What about the children often abandoned to institutions where they have no father or mother, where they suffer so much emotional deprivation and trauma that many become psychotic, neurotic, or so full of hate and violence that they become juvenile delinquents and criminals who kill, rape, and maim? When a person is treated badly in his or her childhood, that inner violence manifests itself when he or she is grown up.

The pro-choice philosophy maintains that the availability of good medical abortions protects the health and fertility of women and allows children to be born into homes where they can receive love, care, affection, and respect for their unique individuality, so that these children grow up to be joyful, loving, caring, responsible members of the community, able to enter into meaningful relationships with others.

> *"The morality of any act cannot be divorced from the foreseeable consequences of that act."*

Thus, reproductive freedom—access to legal abortions, to contraception, and, by extension, to sexual education—protects women and couples and is probably the most important aspect of preventive medicine and psychiatry, as well as the most promising preventative of crime and mental illness in our society. . . .

But probably the biggest benefit of legalized abortion and the one with the greatest impact is that the number of unwanted children is decreasing. Children who are abused, brutalized, or neglected are more likely to become neurotic, psychotic, or criminal elements of society. They become individuals who do not care about themselves or others, who are prone to violence, who are filled with hatred for society and for other people; if the number of such individuals decreases, the welfare of society increases proportionately. . . .

Abortion Liberates Women

Enormous progress has been made in many countries, including the United States and Canada. But in many other countries, legal abortion is still not available. With the beneficial effects of women's access to abortion and reproductive freedom so obvious to so many people, why is there still so much violent opposition to it? I believe it is due to the fact that people who are bound to traditional religious attitudes resent the newly acquired freedom of women and want to turn the clock back.

Taboos and practices regarding human reproduction and sexuality were written into religious teachings hundreds of years ago, which were then written into the laws of the country. Laws on abortion were introduced long before science enlightened us with the facts concerning embryological development. For instance, in the Catholic church it was thought that, at the moment of conception, a fully formed person, termed a homunculus, lived in the mother's womb, and had only to develop to a certain size to be expelled from it. That belief was held in the distant past, but the effect of the imagery still remains, resulting in the Catholic belief that abortion is the murder of a live human being.

Historically, and even up to this day, men hold the authority in all the major religions of the world. In most countries men are also heads of state and lawmakers. In science and medicine, men traditionally hold the reigns of authority and power, only recently allowing women entry into these fields. Is it any wonder then, that laws and attitudes regarding abortion took so long to change? But now these attitudes are changing, and women around the world are gradually acquiring more power and more control of their reproductive capacities. . . .

For those who believe that the so-called pro-life have occupied the high moral ground in the debate on abortion, I say, "Rubbish." They have never been on a high moral ground, they only pretend to occupy this elevated position by cloaking their oppressive beliefs under the lofty rhetoric of "the defense of innocent unborn life" or "the struggle against the death dealing abortion industry" and similar misleading and blatantly false propaganda. As well, the recourse by the anti-choice movement to violence and murder in order to impose their so-called morality on the whole of society certainly robs them of any credibility. . . .

Let us keep in mind the positive accomplishments of reproductive freedom that I mentioned earlier. An abortion need not be a traumatic event; it often is a liberating experience for the woman, who is able to make an important decision in her life, who exercises her right to choose what is best for her. That is the meaning of freedom, of empowerment.

A woman's choice to terminate a pregnancy is both empowering and liberating. It empowers her because her choice acknowledges that she understands her options, her current situation, and her future expectations, and she is able to make a fully informed decision about what would most benefit her and act on it. It liberates her because she can regain control of her reproductive system and chart her destiny without an unwanted child in tow. It liberates her to fully care for her existing family, her career, her emotional and mental well-being, and her goals. . . .

A Better Society Through Abortion

I wish to conclude on a personal note. Over the years many people have asked me: "Why did you decide to expose yourself to so much stress and danger in a controversial cause, and why do you persist in doing so?" The answer, after a great deal of reflecting upon it, is the following:

I am a survivor of the Nazi Holocaust, that orgy of cruelty and inhumanity of man to man. As such, I have personally experienced suffering, oppression, and injustice inflicted by men beholden to an inhuman, dogmatic, irrational ideology. To relieve suffering, to diminish oppression and injustice, is very important to me. Reproductive freedom and good access to medical abortion means that women can give life to wanted babies at a time when they can provide love, care, and nurturing. Well-loved children grow into adults who do not build concentration camps, do not rape, and do not murder. They are likely to enjoy life, to love and care for each other and the larger society.

> *"Good access to medical abortion means that women can give life to wanted babies at a time when they can provide love, care, and nurturing."*

By fighting for reproductive freedom, I am contributing to a more caring and loving society based on the ideals of peace, justice and freedom, and devoted to the full realization of human potential. Having known myself the depth of human depravity and cruelty, I wish to do whatever I can to replace hate with love, cruelty with kindness, and irrationality with reason.

This is why I am so passionately dedicated to the cause I defend and why I will continue to promote it as long as I have a valid contribution to offer.

Abortion Is Not Murder

by Miriam Claire

About the author: *Miriam Claire is the author of* The Abortion Dilemma: Personal Views on a Public Issue.

Abortion providers in the United States, along with their staff, patients, and volunteer escorts, are being terrorized by people who charge that they are "killing babies." Although there is opposition to abortion in other countries, protests rarely turn violent. Why are some Americans so passionate in their hatred of abortion and all associated with it that they are willing to murder? Is it because they are more moral than the rest of us? Are they alone privy to God's will? I doubt it.

Expert "marketing" of the notion that abortion is murder, via the pulpit and media, is responsible for the current hysterical antiabortion crusades in the United States. According to Frances Kissling, president of the Washington, D.C.–based organization Catholics for a Free Choice, "Catholic bishops were not particularly active on the abortion issue until it became legal in 1973. Then they immediately geared up for a campaign to recriminalize abortion.". . .

Marketing is the antiabortion conspirators' most deadly weapon. Human Life International distributes a variety of antiabortion pamphlets, as well as posters and plastic fetus dolls. A pamphlet that proclaims "Abortion is the Greatest War of All Time" is among the most widely distributed throughout the nationwide network of antiabortion publications. Father Matthew Habiger leads Human Life International's crusade against abortion. He calls clinics death camps and death mills and describes abortion as a holocaust. He is proud of his work and does not believe that the language of his publications is inflammatory. If that kind of inference is not inflammatory, I don't know what is! . . .

A Legal Definition

Antiabortion protesters define murder in an absolute sense as morally wrongful killing, disregarding the legal meaning of the word. In all of the dictionary definitions of murder that I have read, the words *intentional* and *unlawful* appear in one form or another. In many definitions, including the one contained in the 1973 *Unabridged Random House Dictionary of the English Language,* murder is defined as the *"unlawful killing* of another *human being* with malice *aforethought"* or something similar. The word *unlawful* is very important, because it implies that killing IS lawful in some circumstances, but when it is unlawful, it becomes murder. Premeditation, unlawfulness, and a human being as victim are the three elements that define murder.

Premeditation definitely pertains to abortion because in one way or another the woman decides to have an abortion and takes steps to carry it out. That is by any definition intentional behavior.

Unlawfulness is a far more complex element, because laws change according to the views of a majority of people or as a result of a few imposing their will on a majority, regardless of whether there is evidence to substantiate them. At present, abortion is lawful in many countries, including the United States, and unlawful in others. There are states within the United States such as Utah, North Dakota, and Kansas, where it is extremely difficult to have an abortion despite *Roe v. Wade*, because of restrictive state laws and lack of providers. . . .

If we define abortion as murder according to its legality, the moral definition becomes absurd, because historically laws have been changed as a result of a whole series of factors and views unrelated to the fetus and morality. Lawfulness does not provide an acceptable, consistent standard by which to measure whether abortion is morally wrongful killing. Abortion can change its legal status from minute to minute, but murder cannot change its definition. If language is to have any meaning at all, the definition has to be precise and consistent.

The third element needed to define killing as "murder" is a human being, according to the majority of dictionary definitions. Almost all people who feel that abortion is murder believe that the fetus is a human being from the moment of conception, or from some time soon after conception, and that it has all of the feelings and rights of a born human being. It is a belief that has been the subject of debate among scholars, the clergy, and lay persons for centuries, because the definition of a human being is very elusive.

It is important to understand that the belief that the fetus is a human being from the moment of conception cannot be substantiated by any scientific or biological evidence. A belief by definition requires a leap of faith, precisely because there is no valid evidence to prove it. If enough people collectively believe, that doesn't convert the belief into a fact, although the communal feeling may become

> *"Abortion can change its legal status from minute to minute, but murder cannot change its definition."*

manifest in laws and religion. Just because more than 50% of the American people (according to various polls) believe that abortion is murder doesn't make it true. Many of those same people also believe that abortion is justified in some cases, especially rape and incest, and should be legally available. If abortion is murder, why should there be exceptions to a law against it?

A Scientific Understanding

The various religious views on abortion will not be discussed, for they will not in any way help answer the question "Is abortion murder?" Religion is highly relevant to a personal quest for moral answers, but it cannot serve as a basis for laws in a pluralistic society. If we are to find a foundation on which to formulate laws that will satisfy the consciences of people of all religions, biological fact must be accepted as the only valid evidence to prove, or disprove, that the fetus is a thinking, feeling human being, because it presents some form of objective criteria.

Physicians and neuroscientists are the only professionals suitably qualified to provide biological evidence that will be useful in determining whether the fetus is a human being and hence whether abortion is murder. Of course the way physicians and scientists observe and interpret biological data is not universally consistent, but we must start somewhere, and they have the scientific knowledge that we need to build our legal foundation.

I was privileged to conduct the last extensive interview with the late Dr. Bertram Wainer, founder/director of one of the first abortion clinics in the world, the Fertility Control Clinic in Melbourne, Australia. Dr. Wainer made tremendous personal sacrifices, suffered financial ruin, and risked his

> *"If abortion is murder, why should there be exceptions to a law against it?"*

life to help secure Australian women the right to have a safe abortion. All quotes attributed to Dr. Wainer are excerpts from that interview.

> When does human life become a human person? What value shall be accorded to the fetus? I think about it all the time. We all do at the Clinic. Yes, I'm concerned. . . . It would be a much more comfortable world if we didn't have to make decisions about abortions. At no time have I said that the fetus is zilch.

Dr. Wainer's recognition that the fetus is more than "zilch" encapsulates the essence of the problem in determining whether abortion is murder. Biologically, what is the fetus?

When I interviewed Dr. Henry Morgentaler, founder/director of the first abortion clinic in Canada, he reflected that

> Unfortunately, most of the people who are against abortion do not seem able to make the distinction between potential life and a real live baby. When you go on the assumption that a fertilized egg is already a baby, which is completely crazy and nonscientific, then you have to be blinded by dogma not to understand that a microscopic cell is not a baby.

The growth from a microscopic cell to a baby takes nine months. Even among physicians there are differences of opinion about when the multiplying cells have turned into a baby, which is one reason why most physicians prefer to perform abortions early in pregnancy, in the first 12 weeks.

Dr. Bernard Nathanson, formerly the head of the largest abortion clinic in the United States and founder of NARAL [National Abortion Rights Action League], an organization that helped bring about the legalization of abortion in the United States, is against abortion now

> because the development of medical technology has given us a far greater insight into the life of the fetus which is a human being, biologically and scientifically. Abortion is the destruction of that life. I don't think that we can afford to engage ourselves in a program of killing of what the Nazi doctors used to call "lebens unwertes leben"—life unworthy of living. That was the motto of the Nazi extermination program. It is what we have been doing here in the United States.

That argument is based on the belief that the fetus is a human being from the moment of conception. . . .

Justified Killing

Without the three elements that define murder as murder, killing is not murder, however much we hate it. Killing, though sad and undesirable, is not always morally wrong. If the mother's life is threatened in the third trimester, then a choice might have to be made between the mother's life and the unborn, possibly viable human being's life if a cesarean section is not possible (extremely rare). That would be a sad and tragic choice to have to make, but the arguments in favor of saving the mother's life are very potent, because she has a history of relationships and emotional ties which the unborn does not. She also has a better chance of survival than a premature baby.

A helpful definition of abortion appeared in the book *Abortion* by Malcolm Potts, Peter Diggory, and John Peel. They define it as

> the loss of a pregnancy before the fetus or fetuses are potentially capable of life independent of the mother. In most mammals, this period extends roughly over the first two-thirds of the pregnancy.

This definition is acceptable to me because it covers the first two trimesters prior to synaptic connections in the brain. The term *abortion* is inappropriate for third-trimester terminations because the procedure at that stage falls into the category of mercy killing and a different set of criteria apply.

A popular book among those against abortion is *The Abortion Holocaust: Today's Final Solution* by William Brennan. [Holocaust survivor] Dr. Henry Morgentaler's response to this comparison of the Holocaust with abortion is that

> it is dishonest. There's simply no comparison between what took place in the concentration camps and what takes place during an abortion. Hopefully, reason will prevail. We have an era of unreason now with evangelists preaching simple things. But I suppose if you accept the premise that a fetus is a human

being from the moment of conception, then I guess you would be justified in talking about the killing of innocent human beings and making comparisons with the Holocaust and murder. But if that premise is wrong, then everything else is wrong. I simply don't accept that premise. It's based on a fallacy and an arbitrary dogma. A human body is made up of millions of cells, not just one or a few. The pictures presented in the book *The Abortion Holocaust* portray a 24-week-old fetus—not all, or even many, abortions are performed at that stage.

To say that a human being exists from the moment of conception is absurd from a biological standpoint. It's simply not true. What does exist is the potential for a human being to develop during the next nine months.

While Dr. Morgentaler was in prison, a fellow prisoner asked him how he could justify killing babies. Dr. Morgentaler replied:

They are not babies. If they were, I would not be performing abortions. . . . A woman who wants an abortion doesn't want to kill a baby. She doesn't want the product of conception to become a baby.

No abortion providers anywhere in the world have told me that they would be willing to kill a baby. All have expressed one main reason for performing abortions: to protect women from being butchered and give them the option of a safe abortion. . . .

Killing Is Not Murder

Of the three elements necessary to define abortion as murder—premeditation, unlawfulness, and a human being—only premeditation can be reasonably and consistently described as an integral aspect of abortion. Unlawfulness tells us whether abortion is illegal, but not if it is morally wrongful killing, because history has shown that abortion has been made illegal for a variety of reasons that have no relationship to morality. Thinking, feeling, awareness, and an ability to experience pain are key elements of personhood, but the brain development of a fetus is not sufficient to respond in these ways until around 28 weeks of gestation. Abortion in the first and second trimesters cannot be defined as murder because the fetus is not a person in the sense that we understand personhood at that stage in pregnancy.

In the third trimester, lawfulness becomes the key element that would determine whether abortion is murder. If we decide that saving the mother's life or preventing a very crippled fetus from being born a severely crippled baby are insufficient reasons to terminate a pregnancy and we ban all late abortions, then abortion might well be considered murder in the third trimester, because there is a potentially viable human being *in utero*. If we decide that these circumstances would justify a late abortion, then termination in the third trimester would not

> *"Of the three elements necessary to define abortion as murder . . . only premeditation . . . [is] an integral aspect of abortion."*

be murder because it would be a lawful procedure, but it would be killing a possibly viable, developing human being, for which we must be willing to take responsibility. My feeling is that third-trimester terminations should be permitted to save the mother's life only if a vaginal delivery or cesarean section is not possible. If the fetus is fatally ill or severely crippled, then termination would be justified in my view, but I would call it euthanasia, not abortion. Those scenarios are extremely rare, but possible. Abortion should not be permitted in the third trimester for any other reason.

> *"Abortion kills the potential for a fetus to fully develop, but that is **not murder.**"*

The product of conception is alive and undeniably made up of living cells, and after an abortion the form those cells take—an embryo or fetus—is dead. Any living thing will die when removed from its source of sustenance, and that, by any definition, is killing. Abortion kills the potential for a fetus to fully develop, but that is *not* murder, because it is not killing an actual human being.

The Bible Does Not Condemn Abortion

by Freedom from Religion Foundation

About the author: *The Freedom from Religion Foundation works to promote the separation of church and state and to educate the public about nontheistic beliefs.*

What does the Bible say about abortion? Absolutely nothing! The word "abortion" does not appear in any translation of the bible!

Out of more than 600 laws of Moses, none comments on abortion. One Mosaic law about miscarriage specifically contradicts the claim that the Bible is antiabortion, clearly stating that miscarriage does not involve the death of a human being. If a woman has a miscarriage as the result of a fight, the man who caused it should be fined. If the woman dies, however, the culprit must be killed:

> If men strive, and hurt a woman with child, so that her fruit depart from her, and yet no mischief follow: he shall be surely punished according as the woman's husband will lay upon him; and he shall pay as the judges determine.
>
> And if any mischief follow, then thou shalt give life for life, eye for eye, tooth for tooth . . . —*Ex. 21:22–25*

The bible orders the death penalty for murder of a human being, but not for the expulsion of a fetus.

When Does Life Begin?

According to the Bible, life begins at birth—when a baby draws its first breath. The Bible defines life as "breath" in several significant passages, including the story of Adam's creation in Genesis 2:7, when God "breathed into his nostrils the breath of life; and man became a living soul." Jewish law traditionally considers that personhood begins at birth.

Desperate for a biblical basis for their beliefs, some antiabortionists cite obscure passages, usually metaphors or poetic phrasing, such as: "Behold, I was shapen in iniquity; and in sin did my mother conceive me." (Psalm 51:5) This

Excerpted from "What Does the Bible Say About Abortion?" an online article from Freedom from Religion Foundation at www.infidels.org/org/ffrf/nontracts/abortion.html. Reprinted with permission from Freedom from Religion Foundation, Inc.

is sexist, but does nothing other than to invoke original sin. It says nothing about abortion.

The Commandments, Moses, Jesus and Paul ignored every chance to condemn abortion. If abortion was an important concern, why didn't the bible say so?

Thou Shalt Not Kill?

Many antiabortionists quote the sixth commandment, "Thou shalt not kill" (Ex. 20:13) as evidence that the bible is antiabortion. They fail to investigate the bible's definition of life (breath) or its deafening silence on abortion. Moreover, the Mosaic law in Exodus 21:22–25, directly following the Ten Commandments, makes it clear that an embryo or fetus is not a human being.

An honest reader must admit that the bible contradicts itself. "Thou shalt not kill" did not apply to many living, breathing human beings, including children, who are routinely massacred in the bible. The Mosaic law orders "Thou shalt kill" people for committing such "crimes" as cursing one's father or mother (Ex. 21:17), for being a "stubborn son" (Deut. 21:18–21), for being a homosexual (Lev. 20:13), or

> *"The bible orders the death penalty for murder of a human being, but not for the expulsion of a fetus."*

even for picking up sticks on the Sabbath (Numbers 15:32–35)! Far from protecting the sanctity of life, the bible promotes capital punishment for conduct which no civilized person or nation would regard as criminal.

Mass killings were routinely ordered, committed or approved by the God of the bible. One typical example is Numbers 25:4–9, when the Lord casually orders Moses to massacre 24,000 Israelites: "Take all the heads of the people, and hang them up before the Lord against the sun." Clearly, the bible is not pro-life!

Most scholars and translators agree that the injunction against killing forbade only the murder of (already born) Hebrews. It was open season on everyone else, including children, pregnant women and newborn babies.

Does God Kill Babies?

"Happy shall he be, that taketh and dasheth thy little ones against the stones."—*Psalm 137:9*

The bible is not pro-child. Why did God set a bear upon 42 children just for teasing a prophet (2 Kings 2:23–24)? Far from demonstrating a "pro-life" attitude, the bible decimates innocent babies and pregnant women in passage after gory passage, starting with the flood and the wanton destruction of Sodom and Gomorrah, progressing to the murder of the firstborn child of every household in Egypt (Ex. 12:29), and the New Testament threats of annihilation.

Space permits only a small sampling of biblical commandments or threats to kill children:

• *Numbers 31:17* Now therefore kill every male among the little ones.

- *Deuteronomy 2:34* utterly destroyed the men and the women and the little ones.
- *Deuteronomy 28:53* And thou shalt eat the fruit of thine own body, the flesh of thy sons and of thy daughters.
- *I Samuel 15:3* slay both man and woman, infant and suckling.
- *2 Kings 8:12* dash their children, and rip up their women with child.
- *2 Kings 15:16* all the women therein that were with child he ripped up.
- *Isaiah 13:16* Their children also shall be dashed to pieces before their eyes; their houses shall be spoiled and their wives ravished.
- *Isaiah 13:18* They shall have no pity on the fruit of the womb; their eyes shall not spare children.
- *Lamentations 2:20* Shall the women eat their fruit, and children.
- *Ezekiel 9:6* Slay utterly old and young, both maids and little children.
- *Hosea 9:14* give them a miscarrying womb and dry breasts.
- *Hosea 13:16* their infants shall be dashed in pieces, and their women with child shall be ripped up.

Then there are the dire warnings of Jesus in the New Testament:

> "For, behold, the days are coming, in which they shall say, Blessed are the barren, and the womb that never bare, and the paps which never gave suck."—*Luke 23:29*

The teachings and contradictions of the bible show that antiabortionists do not have a "scriptural base" for their claim that their deity is "pro-life." Spontaneous abortions occur far more often than medical abortions. Gynecology textbooks conservatively cite a 15% miscarriage rate, with one medical study finding a spontaneous abortion rate of almost 90% in very early pregnancy. That would make a deity in charge of nature the greatest abortionist in history!

Are Bible Teachings Kind to Women?

The bible is neither antiabortion nor pro-life, but does provide a biblical basis for the real motivation behind the antiabortion religious crusade: hatred of women. The bible is anti-woman, blaming women for sin, demanding subservience, mandating a slave/master relationship to men, and demonstrating contempt and lack of compassion:

> "I will greatly multiply thy sorrow and thy conception; in sorrow thou shalt bring forth children; and thy desire shall be to thy husband, and he shall rule over thee."—*Genesis 3:16*

What self-respecting woman today would submit willingly to such tyranny?

The antiabortion position does not demonstrate love for humanity, or compassion for real human beings. Worldwatch Institute statistics show that 50% of abortions worldwide are illegal, and that at least 200,000 women die every year—and thousands more are hurt and maimed—from illegal or self-induced abortions. Unwanted pregnancies and complications from multiple pregnancies are a leading killer of women. Why do antiabortionists want North American women to join these ghastly mortality statistics? Every day around the world more than 40,000 people, mostly children, die from starvation or malnutrition. We must protect and cherish the right to life of the already-born. . . .

Belief that "a human being exists at conception" is a matter of faith, not fact. Legislating antiabortion faith would be as immoral and unAmerican as passing a law that all citizens must attend Catholic mass!

The bible does not condemn abortion; but even if it did, we live under a secular constitution, not in a theocracy. The separation of church and state, the right to privacy, and women's rights all demand freedom of choice.

Chapter 2

Should Abortion Rights Be Protected or Restricted?

Chapter Preface

When seventeen-year-old Becky Bell of Indianapolis learned that she was preg-nant in 1988, she decided to have an abortion without telling her parents. How-ever, because Indiana law requires a minor to have her parents' consent before she can have an abortion, Becky's options were limited: She could have appeared be-fore a judge to request a judicial bypass, which would have allowed her to obtain an abortion without her parents' knowledge; she could have traveled 110 miles to neighboring Kentucky, which did not have a parental consent law; or she could have tried to obtain an abortion from a less reputable clinic in her home state—one willing to break the law. Becky chose an illegal abortion. Less than a week later she was dead, some say due to complications from the abortion.

Abortion rights supporters often use Becky Bell as an example of the dangers of parental consent and notification laws. Currently, twenty-two states have laws that require a teen to notify or obtain consent from either one or both of her parents, with judicial bypass as an alternative. But critics of such laws argue that judicial bypass is not a viable option for most teens, who either have little knowledge of the legal system or are frequently too intimidated to appear before a judge. Like-wise, they maintain, a teen must often wait weeks or longer to obtain a judicial bypass, which makes an abortion riskier for her. Furthermore, abortion rights sup-porters fear that legislation such as the Child Custody Protection Act, a bill that would prohibit any adult other than a teen's parents from taking her across state lines for an abortion, would only compound the already difficult situation. (The bill has not yet been passed by Congress.) If Becky Bell had had transportation to Kentucky, they argue, she could have received a safe, legal abortion.

Supporters of parental consent and notification laws contend, however, that these laws are vital to protecting the health and welfare of young women. They maintain that notification laws protect a teen by ensuring that her parents can monitor her health and mental well-being both before and after her abortion. Supporters assert that if Becky Bell's parents had been notified of her abortion, they would have sought medical attention for her complications much sooner and perhaps saved her life. As California politician John Pinkerton comments, "Parents must give consent before their child can have their ears pierced or a tattoo put on. . . . It is outrageous to allow a child to undergo any surgical pro-cedure, let alone an invasive, irreversible procedure such as an abortion, with-out parental notification."

As more and more states enact parental involvement laws and Congress con-siders federal legislation, the debate over a woman's constitutional right to abortion will likely gain momentum. In the following chapter, the authors ex-amine whether abortion rights should be protected or restricted.

Restricting Abortion Would Be Destructive to Families

by Jerry Z. Muller

About the author: *Historian Jerry Z. Muller is the author of numerous books concerning social and political history.*

In contemporary American political debate, struggles over abortion are usually treated as conflicts between rival interpretations of individual rights. Those who favor abortion most often invoke the "right to choose" of the woman who has conceived the fetus. Those who oppose abortion focus on the "right to life" of the fetus. But there is a third position that is largely overlooked. Essentially conservative and "pro-family," it favors abortion as the right choice to promote healthy family life under certain circumstances.

This argument, which emphasizes the social function of the family over the rights of the individual, begins with the assumption that the possibility of choice matters less than the choices made. It argues that the choice to give birth to a child isn't always the right one. In fact, under some conditions, choosing to give birth may be socially dysfunctional, morally irresponsible or even cruel: inimical to the forces of stability and bourgeois responsibility conservatives cherish.

Supporters of middle-class family values may agree with many Christian Coalition positions. They may advocate raising the income-tax deduction for dependent children, question the legitimation of homosexuality and condemn violence and sex in the cultural marketplace. But the right-to-life position undermines their fundamentally conservative effort to strengthen purposeful families. For the right-to-life position requires massive government intrusion into the most intimate of realms, removes decisions about whether to bear children from those who are to raise them and threatens what many conservatives regard as the most significant mediating institution in modern capitalist society, the family. The success of the right-to-life position would lead almost inevitably to an increase in the number of children born into socially dysfunctional settings.

Right-to-Life Ideology

The prime obstacle to the right-to-life movement is not feminism. It is the millions of more or less conservative middle-class parents who know that, if their teenage daughter were to become pregnant, they would advise her to get an abortion rather than marry out of necessity or go through the trauma of giving birth and then placing the child up for adoption. Many people—young, unmarried, pregnant women loath to bring a child into a family-less environment; parents of a fetus known to be afflicted by a disease such as Tay-Sachs that will make its life painful and short; parents whose children are likely to be born with severe genetic defects, who know that the birth of the fetus will mean pain for them and for their other children—all choose abortion, not because they fetishize choice but

> *"Under some conditions, choosing to give birth may be socially dysfunctional, morally irresponsible or even cruel."*

because they value the family. Many couples who know that their offspring will be at risk for genetic diseases and other birth defects owe their actual families to abortion: were it not for the possibility of detecting these diseases in utero and of aborting stricken fetuses, such couples would not risk having children at all.

The right-to-life movement regards human "life" as a good—a claim most of us are broadly inclined to accept. But the right-to-life movement goes further. It regards all human life as a good, regardless of the mental, emotional or intellectual capacities of the individual. To right-to-lifers, keeping alive anencephalic infants (children missing all or most of their brains) is a moral imperative. The right-to-life movement regards every degree of human life as equal to the most complete development of human life: that is why the moral status of a fetus two weeks into its development is the same as that of children and adults.

For the right-to-life movement, then, human life is not only a good, it is the highest good, and it is always the highest good. The movement's strategic aim is to extend state power to preserve and protect every fetus that is conceived, regardless of the circumstances under which it is conceived, regardless of the condition of the fetus and regardless of the will of the fetus's parents.

Family Preservation

The right-to-life movement has done our society a service by insisting upon the humanity and moral worth of the unborn child. But opponents of abortion have turned a legitimate moral concern into a moral absolute. They have made biological life not one good to be fought for, but the only good, to which all others must be subordinated. For this reason, anti-abortion activists insist that abortion be forbidden in cases of rape or incest: to suggest there are moral considerations other than those of the life of the fetus is to question the fundamental premises of the right-to-life movement.

One of those considerations is the creation and preservation of families. The pro-life movement is at odds with the assumptions of middle-class family formation. These families believe that the bearing and rearing of children is not an inexorable fate but a voluntary vocation, and that, like any other vocation, it is to be pursued methodically using the most effective means available. Such a conception of the family includes planning when children are to be born and how many are to be born. It seeks to increase the chances of successfully socializing and educating children in order to help them find fulfilling work and spiritual lives. The number of children is kept low in part because the amount of parental time and resources devoted to raising them is expected to be high. . . .

The technological repertoire of today's family planning includes abortion to prevent out-of-wedlock childbirth, artificial contraception within marriage and voluntary sterilization when families have reached their desired size. This activist conception of family formation also suggests that artificial reproductive technology should be used to reverse infertility. Prenatal screening is part of the package: potential children known to carry debilitating diseases may be aborted to make possible the birth of children more likely to grow into healthy, productive adulthood. Given the assumptions of middle-class family formation, ignoring such technological possibilities can even be regarded as a form of child neglect.

> *"Potential children known to carry debilitating diseases may be aborted to make possible the birth of children more likely to grow into healthy, productive adulthood."*

This middle-class vision of the family is linked to other elements of modern life. It is a conception that those who seek to conserve modern society ought to fortify rather than undermine. It is under attack from many quarters, including the individualism and hedonism of much of our popular and elite culture and the emphasis on career advancement among both men and women. But it is also threatened from another direction by the right-to-life movement. . . .

The Socializing Influence of Families

The ideology of middle-class family formation maintains that families are not just another lifestyle option but an essential part of a modern society. Illegitimacy is stigmatized because it is socially dysfunctional. Conservatives have long assumed that government should promote those social norms that encourage the creation of decent men and women and discourage those that experience has shown to be harmful. This logic lies at the heart of conservative debates on public policy, including recent proposals to reform welfare to discourage out-of-wedlock births.

The right-to-life movement stands as a barrier to such reform. The removal of government subsidies for the bearing of out-of-wedlock children, it is said, will create an incentive for pregnant teenagers and other pregnant unmarried women to resort more frequently to abortion. Though the claim is most often articulated by pro-life opponents of welfare reform, it is also an unarticulated premise of many who favor the elimination of welfare payments to unwed mothers.

Is it more important to minimize abortion or to minimize the birth of children to women who are unprepared to provide the familial structure needed for children to become stable and responsible adults? A

> *"Is it more important to minimize abortion or to minimize the birth of children to women who are unprepared to provide familial structure?"*

growing consensus holds that unsocialized children are at the heart of our social deterioration, not only because they are more likely to engage in violent and criminal activity, but because they lack the discipline needed to learn in school and to function in the workplace. The socializing influence of the family—comprising husbands and wives in ongoing union and with a commitment to child-rearing—appears to be an essential element of any solution. If these assumptions are correct, as conservatives and many liberals now believe, the trade-off is more biological lives at the cost of more unsocialized children—making people versus making people moral.

Out-of-Wedlock Births

Opposition to the elimination of welfare payments for out-of-wedlock children comes from two quarters: the pro-choice movement and the right-to-life movement. The former condemns "welfare caps" because they reduce the choices facing women, and all choices are to be protected. In the words of liberal feminist Iris Young, "A liberal society that claims to respect the autonomy of all its citizens equally should affirm the freedom of all citizens to bear and rear children, whether they are married or not, whether they have high incomes or not." For the right-to-life movement, of course, no fact about the potentially miserable outcome of the fetus's birth affects the imperative that it be born. Beginning from different commitments, therefore, feminists and pro-lifers converge in rejecting the conservative assumption that the troubling social effects of out-of-wedlock births justify government attempts to limit them.

The current right-to-life strategy calls for "chipping away" at the liberal abortion culture to "save" as many babies as possible under the political circumstances. Because pro-lifers can have the greatest impact on legislation affecting the poor, the socially marginal and those dependent on governmental funding for medical procedures, among their first targets have been, for example, Medicaid recipients. As a result, the success of the pro-life movement is now measured in the lives of poor children born out of wedlock. Most abortions in the U.S. occur to avoid the birth of children out of wedlock. Of the roughly 1.5 million abortions in 1991, only 271,000 were performed upon married women.

Among married women, there were eight abortions for every ninety births; among unmarried women, there were forty-eight abortions for every forty-five births. All else being equal, then, eliminating the possibility of abortion would hike the number of out-of-wedlock births from its already disastrous level of 30 percent to 49 percent.

Indeed, the anti-abortion movement may already have helped increase the number of children born out of wedlock. The percentage of out-of-wedlock births in the United States rose from 18.4 percent in 1980 to 30.1 percent of all births in 1992, according to recent reports from the National Center for Health Statistics. During the same period, the proportion of non-marital pregnancies ending in abortion declined, from 60 percent in 1980 to 46 percent in 1991, and the abortion rate among unmarried women fell by 12 percent.

Thirty percent of these mothers were teenagers. The statistics on all potential mothers aged 15 to 17, those least able to care adequately for their children, are more alarming still. In the years from 1986 to 1991 the pregnancy rate for this group rose by 7 percent, but the abortion rate dropped by 19 percent, so that the rate of out-of-wedlock births among these very young mothers increased by 27 percent. This trend toward out-of-wedlock births rather than abortion may be due either to the increased difficulty of obtaining abortions or to increased preference for carrying babies to term. Either way, it marks a partial victory for the pro-life movement.

To focus on the conflict between the right-to-life movement and middle-class family values is to call into question the terms in which the abortion debate is usually cast in our political culture. The abortion struggle should be understood as a three-way debate: among liberals, who believe that to let each of us do as we like will work out for the best; pro-

> *"Eliminating the possibility of abortion would hike the number of out-of-wedlock births from its already disastrous level."*

lifers, who cling to one ultimate good at the expense of all others; and those committed to conserving middle-class families, sometimes at the expense of "choice," sometimes at the expense of "life." The third group lays best claim to the title "conservative."

Teen Access to Abortion Should Not Be Restricted

by Planned Parenthood

About the author: *Planned Parenthood is a family planning organization that works to secure access to abortion and protects reproductive rights. The organization presented this testimony before Congress during hearings about the Child Custody Protection Act, H.R. 1218, which prohibits taking minors across state lines in order to circumvent state laws that require parental notification or consent for an abortion. The bill has not passed.*

Planned Parenthood Federation of America opposes H.R. 1218 [the Child Custody Protection Act]. This bill sends the harsh message to young women facing unintended pregnancies that they cannot turn for help to responsible adults. As such, it seriously obstructs the ability of young women to obtain safe and legal abortions, and puts them and any responsible adults who attempt to assist them at additional risk when they exercise their constitutional right to do so.

Extending the Reach of Government

This bill would make it a federal crime for anyone except a parent to assist a young woman by "transporting" her across state lines for an abortion unless she first complies with her home state's parental involvement law. This is so even if the receiving state does not similarly require parental involvement. Under existing law, state laws mandating parental involvement do not apply to abortions performed in another state, nor is it a crime in any state for a minor to cross state lines to obtain an abortion. H.R. 1218 attempts to change this by extending the reach of state parental involvement laws across state borders to apply any time anyone but a parent drives a young woman out of state for an abortion.

Therefore, the bill would interfere with the deliberate policy choices of some state legislatures by creating a federal mandate that young women obtain parental consent or notification for abortion even in states that have chosen not to impose such requirements, or that impose less restrictive laws than neighboring states. For example, North Carolina allows a grandparent to consent to a

Excerpted from Planned Parenthood, *Child Custody Protection Act: Hearings on H.R. 1218*, 106th Congress, 1st session, congressional testimony before the U.S. House Committee on the Judiciary, Subcommittee on the Constitution, May 27, 1999.

minor's abortion, while Virginia requires a parent to be notified before an abortion. Under H.R. 1218, a Virginia grandmother would violate federal law by driving her granddaughter to North Carolina for an abortion without notifying the girl's parents, even though the abortion would be perfectly legal in North Carolina. Moreover, the crime would be committed even if the grandmother was completely unaware of the federal law prohibiting such "transport," or the Virginia law requiring parental notice, and was taking the granddaughter to North Carolina merely because that was the closest place to obtain an abortion.

> *"Young women who are unable to talk with their parents [would be] at risk—and . . . people they turn to for help [would be treated] as criminals."*

Planned Parenthood encourages young women to involve their parents when they face an unintended pregnancy and are considering abortion. Most teenagers do so, even when it is not required by law. The younger the teenager, the more likely it is that she has told her parent. But not every family is a model family. H.R. 1218 would place young women who are unable to talk with their parents at risk—and treat the people they turn to for help as criminals. In defiance of sound public health policy, this legislation would force some young women into isolation at a time when they desperately need help and the counsel of others, and potentially would endanger the health and constitutional rights of young people. For example:

• Emergency medical personnel could be prosecuted for transporting a young woman across state lines to the closest abortion provider even if the abortion was necessary to save her from serious physical harm. (The bill contains an exception only to preserve the life of the minor).

• A family member of the young woman—even one that has primary responsibility for her upbringing but lacks legal guardianship—could be prosecuted for taking her across state lines for an abortion if the parental involvement law in the state-of-residence had not been satisfied.

• If both states had parental involvement laws that provided for an alternative judicial by-pass procedure, a young pregnant woman who was afraid to involve her parents in her abortion decision due to a history of family violence—and perhaps even sexual abuse and incest—might be forced to maneuver through the complexities of two separate legal proceedings in two states with the inevitable delays that would result.

• Most providers urge women to bring someone with them to drive them home from the procedure. Minors seeking out-of-state abortions would be deprived of this assistance if they felt unable to seek assistance from their parents.

Medical Associations Oppose Mandated Parental Consent

As the American Medical Association (AMA) and the American Association of Pediatrics (AAP) have recognized, confidentiality is essential to encouraging young people to seek sensitive medical services and information in a timely fashion. Recognizing that "some minors may, in fact, be physically or emotionally harmed if they are required to involve their parents in the decision to have an abortion," the Council on Ethical and Judicial Affairs of the AMA has concluded that "(b)ecause the need for privacy may be compelling, minors may be driven to desperate measures to maintain the confidentiality of their pregnancies. They may run away from home, obtain a 'back-alley' abortion, or resort to self-abortion." In a 1996 statement by the AAP, that organization recognized both that mandatory parental notification laws "can delay and obstruct the access of pregnant adolescents to timely professional advice and medical care," and "can have adverse effects on both minors and their families. . . . The risks of violence, abuse, coercion, unresolved conflict, and rejection are significant in nonsupportive or dysfunctional families when parents are informed of a pregnancy against the adolescent's considered judgment." For these reasons, the AMA and AAP have opposed laws that mandate parental involvement in a minor's abortion decision.

Isolation Risks and Restricted Access

Young women seek abortion services outside their home state for a variety of reasons. Some do so because the closest abortion provider is across state lines; currently, 86% of counties—home to 32% of women of childbearing age—lack an abortion provider. Others fear being recognized at an abortion provider in their hometown, or the risk that compliance with their home state's parental involvement mandate will result in a loss of anonymity.

The vast majority of young women who visit a health care facility for an abortion are accompanied by someone—a parent, relative, trusted adult, clergy person, or friend. In fact, it is good medical practice for a patient to have someone to escort her home after an abortion procedure. Because most young women do not travel alone to an abortion provider—and many would have no way of reaching them if someone else didn't drive—H.R. 1218 is tantamount to prohibiting many teens from crossing the state border for an abortion even when an out-of-state provider is significantly closer.

> *"Young women seek abortion services outside their home state for a variety of reasons."*

Even those young women who could find a way to reach an out-of-state abortion provider would be harmed by this legislation. Knowing that anyone who helps them travel across state lines to have an abortion could be guilty of a federal offense (if their home state requires parental involvement), many young women would be afraid to involve trusted adults in their decision to terminate a pregnancy—and many adults who would have provided assistance in the past will refuse to do so for fear of prosecution.

For young women affected by this legislation, H.R. 1218 says that if they plan to seek an abortion out of state, they must do so alone—without guidance, advice, or assistance from anyone. By passing H.R. 1218, Congress would be sending a frightening and dangerous message to the young women of this country.

Young women who could obtain abortions despite the obstacles imposed by this legislation are likely to be delayed in obtaining this medical care. Young women who obtain in-state abortions although an out-of-state provider is closer would have to make and carry out potentially extensive travel plans. Those young women who traveled out of state by themselves would be endangered by traveling alone using public transportation at an especially vulnerable time in their lives, and would inevitably be delayed while they made arrangements to travel to an abortion provider on their own. The significance of these delays is evident in the fact that, while abortion is much safer than childbirth, the medical risks of the procedure increase as the pregnancy progresses.

> *"For young women affected by this legislation . . . , if they plan to seek an abortion out of state, they must do so alone."*

H.R. 1218 Would Impose Irrational Criminal Penalties

H.R. 1218 would impose federal criminal penalties on any person other than a parent who takes a young woman across state lines to obtain an abortion if she does not first comply with her home state's parental involvement law. The primary caregiver of a young woman (but who was not named as legal guardian), for example, could be prosecuted for taking her to an out-of-state abortion provider if the minor's home state's law had not been met. For example, a grandparent or other close relative could face criminal charges, as could a minister or close family friend if the home state's law did not—as most states do not—permit such people to authorize a minor's abortion. Because this legislation has no minimum age for prosecution, a young woman's friend who is under eighteen could be charged for driving her to a nearby, but out-of-state, health care facility. Even emergency medical personnel could be prosecuted under this bill for taking a young woman across state lines for an emergency abortion to prevent a very serious maternal health problem that was not life threatening.

Criminal sanctions could be imposed even if the person accompanying the young woman did not know about this federal law or was unaware that her home state required parental involvement for abortion. Given the complex distinctions among various state laws, this could create a trap for even the most well-intentioned relatives, clergy persons or family friends. For example, both North and South Carolina allow a grandparent to consent to a minor's abortion, but North Carolina requires the minor to have lived with the grandparent for six months. A North Carolina grandmother who takes a granddaughter who she does not live with to South Carolina for an abortion is committing a federal crime, even though the abortion is completely legal in South Carolina, and even though the grandmother is unaware of the distinction between the two states' laws. Also, a grandmother might transport her granddaughter from Kentucky, a state with a parental consent abortion law, to Ohio, a state with a parental notice abortion law. Even if the mother of the minor were notified of her daughter's abortion, which would be sufficient in Ohio where the abortion is being performed, the grandmother would still have committed a federal crime because parental consent was not obtained.

An Unconstitutional Law

H.R. 1218 violates the Constitution in two significant respects. First, it interferes with principles of federalism. Second, it creates an "undue burden" on a minor's right to choose to terminate a pregnancy.

One of the benefits that we derive from our citizenship in a nation comprised of fifty separate states is the right to travel from one state to another and be treated the same as the citizens of the state to which we travel. As the Supreme Court stated in its 1999 *Saenz v. Roe* decision, "a citizen of one State who travels in other States, intending to return home at the end of (her) journey, is entitled to enjoy the 'Privileges and Immunities of Citizens in the several States' that (s)he visits." The right to travel, as embodied in the Privileges and Immunities Clause of the United States Constitution, "provides important protections for nonresidents who enter a State . . . to procure medical services . . ." including reproductive health care services. Just as it would be unlawful to prohibit a citizen of one state from traveling to another state where it was legal to purchase certain goods on Sunday, or marry at a certain age, or procure any other good or service that could not have been purchased in the state of residence, it also is unconstitutional to prohibit a citizen of one state to travel to another state—or to accompany someone traveling to another state—to obtain an abortion. Thus, H.R. 1218 is an unconstitutional infringement on the right to travel.

In addition, principles of federalism require that states respect the deliberate policy decisions of their sister states. H.R. 1218 instead is an affront to any

> *"It . . . is unconstitutional to prohibit a citizen of one state to travel to another state . . . to obtain an abortion."*

state that has chosen not to enact parental involvement requirements, or that has chosen to allow adults other than parents to consent or be notified, or that has constructed a bypass procedure that has more liberal proof requirements than that of the state of the minor's residence. Rather than reinforcing comity among states, H.R. 1218 forces the legal requirements of a minor's state of residence onto other states, thereby undermining the mutual respect upon which our system of federalism rests. Second, H.R. 1218 creates an "undue burden" on a minor's right to terminate a pregnancy. The United States Supreme Court has held that the constitutional right to privacy includes a minor's decision to terminate her pregnancy. It also has held that a restriction on access to abortion is unconstitutional if it imposes a "substantial obstacle" to women's ability to terminate their pregnancies. Thus, for example, a state may not impose a blanket parental involvement requirement that allows a parent to veto a young woman's decision to have an abortion. If a state requires a minor to involve her parent, it must also give her the opportunity to "bypass" that mandate by seeking a judicial determination that she is either sufficiently mature to make her own decision or that, even if she is "immature," the proposed abortion is in her "best interests." A state parental consent law without a judicial bypass option is facially unconstitutional. As the Supreme Court has recognized, "(a)ny independent interest the parent may have in the termination of the minor daughter's pregnancy is no more weighty than the right of privacy of the competent minor mature enough to become pregnant."

> *"A restriction on access to abortion is unconstitutional if it imposes a 'substantial obstacle' to women's ability to terminate their pregnancies."*

An attempt to extend state parental involvement laws across state lines will create a host of logistical dilemmas that threaten to render constitutionally required judicial bypass alternatives meaningless. First, since most state statutes that establish procedures for obtaining a judicial bypass apply only when a young woman is seeking an in-state abortion, it is unclear whether these laws confer authority on the courts of a minor's home state to authorize an out-of-state abortion. If the courts of a minor's home state found that they lacked such authority, a minor would be deprived of the constitutionally mandated option of seeking a judicial bypass.

If, on the other hand, the courts of the minor's home state found that they had authority to grant a waiver when the minor intended to obtain the abortion out of state, a different set of problems arises, especially when both the state of residence and the destination state each has a parental involvement requirement. In such a circumstance, even after obtaining a judicial bypass in her state of residence, the minor still would have to go through a second court proceeding in the destination state, either to satisfy that state's bypass procedure or, at the very least, to have her home state's court order recognized as valid. Requiring a young woman to go through two court proceedings in two states prior to obtaining an abortion presents a substantial obstacle to her exercise of the right to choose abortion, and causes unreasonable delay that presents a further risk to her health.

Even assuming that these logistical obstacles can be overcome, H.R. 1218 is likely to be found by the courts to constitute an unconstitutional "undue burden" on the right to choose for several additional reasons. First, this legislation would impose substantial and, thus, unconstitutional—obstacles to abortion for many young women living in states with parental involvement laws and for whom an out-of-state health facility is the closest place to terminate their pregnancies. These barriers to seeking health services include: being forced to travel substantially further to obtain an in-state abortion; being compelled to go out of state for an abortion without any assistance from relatives, trusted adults, or friends; and being left to carry to term or to take desperate measures to end the pregnancy due to an inability to arrange for a safe abortion under these conditions.

Threatening the Health and Rights of Teens

Furthermore, H.R. 1218 lacks a health exception, and, thus, would unconstitutionally jeopardize the health of young women seeking out-of-state abortions. An exception to the criminal penalties imposed by H.R. 1218 exists only when the abortion is "necessary to save the life of a minor because her life was endangered by a physical disorder, physical injury, or physical illness, including a life endangering physical condition caused by or arising from pregnancy itself." No exception is made for transporting a young woman for an out-of-state abortion that is necessary to save her from grave injury short of death. Further, even the exception for life-threatening conditions does not adequately protect young women's lives. By listing specific circumstances in which life-saving abortions are exempted, the legislation clearly implies that other lifesaving abortions are not exempted. In addition, H.R. 1218 would harm young women's health by forcing them to delay seeking in-state or out-of-state abortions, thereby increasing the medical risks of the procedure.

Finally, this bill would impose federal criminal sanctions on those who had no purpose or intention to violate any state law on parental involvement. This absence of a requirement that a person have a criminal state of mind (in legal parlance, "scienter" or "mens rea") is an additional constitutional defect.

> *"[This law] would harm young women's health by forcing them to delay seeking in-state or out-of-state abortions."*

For these reasons, H.R. 1218 is both an unwise exercise of legislative power, but also an unconstitutional one. In fact, H.R 1218 will threaten both the health and the rights of the very teenagers whom it purportedly is designed to protect. Thus, Planned Parenthood urges the defeat of H.R. 1218.

Abortion Rights Harm Society

by *Society*

About the author: Society *is a bimonthly journal devoted to social science issues and research.*

Years after the Supreme Court's *Roe v. Wade* and *Doe v. Bolton* decisions, the conscience of the American people remains deeply troubled by the practice of abortion-on-demand. Because of these two decisions, abortion is legal at any time of pregnancy, for virtually any reason, in every state. This constitutes an almost completely unrestricted private license to judge who will live and who will die.

That America has the most permissive abortion regime among the world's democracies is a betrayal of the classic American promise of justice for all. That is why a new sense of moral concern is stirring throughout our country. That is why millions of Americans have refused to accept the Court's 1992 admonition to stop debating the issue [*Planned Parenthood of Southeastern Pennsylvania v. Casey*].

To those weary of this argument, it may seem that there is nothing more to be said in the matter of abortion. We disagree.

The Impact of Abortion Rights

Survey research tells us that the American people do not want a legal regime of abortion-on-demand, for any reason, at any time during a pregnancy. We believe we have an obligation to employ the arts of democratic persuasion to help reinstitute legal protection for all unborn children.

The extent of the abortion license and its reach into other areas of law and public policy is widely underestimated. We believe that, as citizens of the United States, we have the responsibility to discuss with our fellow citizens the facts of the abortion license and its impact on our common life.

Many women in crisis earnestly seek alternatives to abortion. We believe we ought to encourage those alternatives and help to provide them.

Pro-life service to women in crisis and pro-life advocacy on behalf of legal reform are expressions of our highest ideals as citizens of the United States. We affirm the nobility of the American Democratic experiment in ordered liberty. We affirm the rule of law and the principle of equal protection under the law, even as we work to reform constitutional and statutory law so that the American legal system is, once again, congruent with the Founders' claim that the inalienable right to life is one of the great moral truths on which American democracy rests. We want an America that is open, hospitable, and caring—a community of civic friendship in which neighbors reach out to assist neighbors in distress.

America's Virtue-Deficit

The abortion license has helped to erode the moral foundations of the American civic community. Right now we are not the country we ought to be. That is why our national conscience is troubled. That distress is, to us, a sign of moral vitality. We speak now because we seek to defend the America we love. We speak to promote the cause of an America in which women and men, together, rebuild the fabric of civil society by acknowledging our common responsibility to serve and protect the weakest and most vulnerable among us. We speak for a rebirth of freedom in these United States: a freedom that finds its fulfillment in goodness.

Americans of every race, economic condition, religion, and political persuasion share a common concern today for what some have called a national "virtue-deficit." As a country, we have not paid sufficient attention to nurturing those habits of heart and mind that make democratic self-governance possible and that undergird what the Framers of the Constitution called "civic virtue." We believe that the abortion license is a critical factor in America's virtue-deficit.

Abortion kills 1.5 million innocent human beings in America every year. There is no longer any serious scientific dispute that the unborn child is a human creature who dies violently in the act of abortion. This brute fact is the root of our national distress over the abortion license. Abortion kills: few would now deny that. But in order to defend the private "right" to lethal violence that is the essence of abortion, proponents of the license frequently resort to euphemisms like "products of conception" and "the termination of pregnancy."

> *"The American people do not want a legal regime of abortion-on-demand, for any reason, at any time during a pregnancy."*

The public dialogue is not coarsened by depictions of the reality of abortion. But a coarsening of our common life has taken place: it is evident in the lack of moral revulsion that follows one newspaper's accurate description of an abortion procedure which "breaks . . . apart" the "fetus" before "it" is "suctioned out of the uterus" or "extracted."

The abortion license hurts women. Some (including the narrow Supreme Court majority in the 1992 *Casey* decision) contend that the license is necessary to ensure social and economic gains for women. It is ever more clear, though, that women pay a huge price for abortion. By providing an alleged technological "fix" for unintended pregnancy, the license has encouraged widespread male irresponsibility and predatory male sexual behavior. Abortion-on-demand has given an excuse to men who shirk their responsibilities, claiming that the child they helped to conceive ought to have been aborted, or that the woman who declined to abort may not impose on him any responsibility for her "lifestyle choice."

Fathers have also been harmed and dehumanized by the abortion license. Some watch their child killed against their will; others learn to their distress only much later that a child they would have raised is dead. Even when agreeing to support the abortion decision, fathers, like mothers, suppress their grief, deny their protective instincts, and otherwise damage themselves when they allow the killing of their own children. Abortion contributes to the marginalization of fatherhood in America which many agree is a primary cause of the alarming breakdown of American family life.

The license has thus poisoned relationships between women and men, even as it has done serious harm to the thousands of women who now suffer from the effects of post-abortion grief. The women of America do not need abortion to be full participants in our society. To suggest otherwise

> *"Abortion . . . has helped to erode the moral foundations of the American civic community."*

is to demean women, to further distort relationships between women and men, and to aggravate the difficulties of re-creating in America a community of virtue and mutual responsibility.

A Private "Right" to Lethal Violence

Abortion is not simply a matter of private "choice." Rather, the abortion license cuts to the heart of America's claim to being a law-governed democracy, in which equality before the law is a fundamental principle of justice. The abortion license also threatens the cultural foundations of our democratic political community. For if it becomes a settled matter in American law and in American public morality that there is, in fact, a private "right" to use lethal violence to "solve" personal, family, or social problems, then the claim of American democracy to be an expression of the people's commitment to "establish justice" will be undermined, just as it was when the law claimed the "right" to exclude certain Americans from its full protection on the basis of race. Thus the abortion issue is the crucial civil rights issue of our time.

A sweeping abortion license was defined unilaterally by the Supreme Court without recourse to the normal procedures of democratic debate and legislation.

This in itself wounded American democracy. And the Court's persistent refusal to permit the American people to debate the basic issue of an alleged "right to abortion" in their legislatures continues to damage our democracy by alienating tens of millions of Americans from their institutions of government.

The Court's definition of a "right to abortion"—first enunciated as a "privacy right," then as a "liberty right" under the Fourteenth Amendment has

"Abortion contributes to the marginalization of fatherhood in America."

had other damaging effects. The language of "rights" puts the dilemma of unwanted pregnancy into a legal—adversarial context, pitting mother against child, and even father against mother. But as the common experience of humanity—and, increasingly, the findings of science—demonstrates, what hurts one party in this most intimate of human relationships hurts both parties. The America we seek is an America in which both mother and child are the subjects of our concern and our community's protection. To abuse the language of "rights" in this matter further advances the demeaning practice of reducing all human relationships in America to matters of adversarial adjudication. This is a prescription for democratic decay. For democracy rests on the foundations of civil society, and in a truly civil society, relationships between people have a far richer moral texture than that suggested by adversarial procedure.

An Abuse of Rights

The Court's vain attempt to justify the abortion license in terms of an all-encompassing right of personal autonomy has begun to infect other areas of the law. Thus the "autonomy" logic of the Court's 1992 *Casey* decision is now invoked as a warrant for a constitutional "right" to euthanasia. And if it were followed to its conclusion, this logic would require us to consider such profound human relationships as the bond between husband and wife, or the bond between parents and children, to be nothing more than matters of contract, with the claims of the autonomous individual trumping all other claims. The jurisprudence of the abortion license as a matter of personal autonomy not only sets mother against child; its logic pits wives against husbands and parents against children. Enshrined by the Court to legalize abortion-on-demand, this autonomy logic threatens to give us an America in which the only actors of consequence are the individual and the state; no other community, including the community of husband and wife, or the community of parents and children, will have effective constitutional standing.

The Supreme Court's insistence on a "right" to abortion has had other disturbing effects on our public life. This "right" has been used to justify the abridgment of First Amendment free speech rights, as when sidewalk counselors are threatened with legal penalties for proposing protection and care to women in crisis at the crucial moment of decision outside an abortion clinic.

This "right" has been used by the Federal government to coerce state governments into providing abortions, even when state legislatures or popular referenda have clearly registered the people's unwillingness to use public funds for elective abortions. The abortion "right" has distorted our national health care debate as well as the debate over welfare reform. It has even had an impact on U.S. foreign policy. American attempts to impose the "right" on the rest of the world at the 1994 Cairo world conference on population and the 1995 Beijing world conference on women have been deeply resented by other countries, as have U.S. attempts to promote abortion overseas through foreign aid.

The Court's attempt to define a "right" to abortion has polarized institutions and professions that were once among the bulwarks of American civil society. Professional associations of lawyers, academics, teachers, and civil servants have been divided by attempts to enlist their resources and prestige in support of abortion-on-demand, and in opposition to any effort even to regulate abortion in ways held constitutional by the Supreme Court. The medical profession has been deeply divided over its relationship to the abortion license. That the practice of abortion-on-demand is now widely recognized within the medical community as contradictory to the most deeply held values of the profession of healing is, we believe, a sign of hope. Yet some medical groups now threaten to reverse this trend by coercion—for example, by requiring medical residency programs to teach and perform abortion techniques. There are also disturbing signs of the corrupting influence of the abortion license in other professions. History has been rewritten to provide specious justification for *Roe v. Wade*. The teaching of law has been similarly distorted, as have political theory and political science. Such extremism underlines the unavoidably public character of the abortion license. The abortion license has a perverse Midas quality—it corrupts whatever it touches.

A Common Responsibility

Our goal is simply stated: we seek an America in which every unborn child is protected in law and welcomed in life. Legal reform and cultural renewal must both take place if America is to experience a new birth of the freedom that is ordered to goodness. . . .

> *"Abortion . . . not only sets mother against child; its logic pits wives against husbands and parents against children."*

Means are always available to enable women to overcome the burdens that can accompany pregnancy and child-rearing. There are always alternatives to abortion. The legacy of *Roe v. Wade* involves a massive denial of this truth and a deformation of social attitudes and practice so pervasive that women are actually encouraged to have abortions as the "easier" road to the goals that an unexpected pregnancy appears to threaten. As individuals and as a society, we bear a common responsibility to make sure that all women know that their own physical and spiritual resources, joined to those of a society that truly affirms and welcomes life, are sufficient to overcome whatever obstacles pregnancy and child-rearing may appear to present. Women instinctively know, and we should never deny, that this path will involve sacrifice. But this sacrifice must no longer remain a one-way street. In particular, men must also assume their proper share of the responsibilities that family life—indeed, civilization itself—requires. . . .

Regulations Are Needed

The unborn child in America today enjoys less legal protection than an endangered species of bird in a national forest. In this situation, we believe a broad-based legal and political strategy is essential. . . .

In its 1992 *Planned Parenthood of Southeastern Pennsylvania v. Casey* decision, the Supreme Court agreed that the state of Pennsylvania could regulate the abortion industry in a number of ways. These regulations do not afford any direct legal protection to the unborn child. Yet experience has shown that such regulations—genuine informed consent, waiting periods, parental notification—reduce abortions in a locality, especially when coupled with positive efforts to promote alternatives to abortion and service to women in crisis. A national effort to enact Pennsylvania-type regulations in all fifty states would be a modest but important step toward the America we seek. . . .

> *"The unborn child in America today enjoys less legal protection than an endangered species of bird in a national forest."*

A more enduring means of constitutional reform is a constitutional amendment both reversing the doctrines of *Roe v. Wade* and *Casey* and establishing that the right to life protected by the Fifth and Fourteenth Amendments extends to the unborn child. Such an amendment would have to be ratified by three-fourths of the states: a requirement that underlines the importance of establishing a track record of progressive legal change on behalf of the unborn child at the state and local level.

Even with a constitutional amendment, every path to the protection and welcome we seek for unborn children requires the re-empowerment of the people of the United States and their elected representatives to debate and resolve the specific statutory enactments that will govern the question of abortion. A constitutional amendment, in other words, is not a self-executing instrument that will end the debate on abortion. It will, rather, correct a gross misinterpretation of the Constitution . . . and require states to debate and adopt policies that do not violate the unborn child's right to life.

Such a process does not, we emphasize, amount to the determination of moral truth by majority rule. Rather, it requires conforming fundamental constitutional principle to a fundamental moral truth—that abortion is the unwarranted taking of an innocent human life. Such a process also respects the role of representative government in fashioning policies that will ultimately secure that principle in practice. The project of constitutional reform on this issue . . . is to bring our legal system into congruence with basic moral truths about the human person.

We believe the pro-life cause is an expression of the premise and promise of American democracy. The premise is that we are all created equal; the promise is that there is justice for all. For all the reasons cited above, the abortion license has done grave damage to America: it has killed tens of millions of unborn children, caused untold anguish to their mothers, and marginalized fathers in our society. The renewal of American democracy according to the highest ideals of the Founders requires us to stand for the inalienable right-to-life of the unborn, to stand with women in crisis, and to stand against the abortion license.

> *"The renewal of American democracy . . . requires us to stand for the inalienable right-to-life of the unborn."*

Few Americans celebrate the abortion license today. For many who are troubled by the license and its impact on our society, to be "reluctantly pro-choice" is now thought to be the responsible position. We respectfully urge those of our neighbors who hold that position to reconsider. We ask them to ponder the relationship between the abortion license and the crisis of family life in America. We ask them to reconsider whether radical autonomy is a sufficient understanding of freedom. We ask them to reflect, again, on the morality of abortion itself. We ask them to think about the social impact of a legally defined private "right" to lethal violence.

We ask them to ask themselves: "Is American society, today, more hospitable, caring, and responsible than it was before *Roe v. Wade*?" We believe the answer is "No." Problems that the proponents of abortion claimed the license would help alleviate—such as childhood poverty, illegitimacy, and child abuse—have in fact gotten worse, throughout every level of our society, since *Roe v. Wade*. Thus we respectfully ask our neighbors to consider the possibility of a connection—cultural as well as legal—between the virtue-deficit in contemporary American life and the abortion license.

Teen Access to Abortion Should Be Restricted

by Mike Fisher

About the author: *Mike Fisher is the attorney general for Pennsylvania. He presented this testimony before the Senate Judiciary Committee during hearings about the Child Custody Protection Act.*

Imagine that you are a divorced mother working hard to raise your children—to ensure they stay in school, stay away from drugs and alcohol and learn the difference between right and wrong. You awake early one morning to find a note left by your barely teenage daughter. You know something is wrong. You check with the neighbors. You call her friends' parents. You call her school only to learn that she is not there. Finally, you call the police. No one knows where your daughter is or what happened to her.

That evening she returns home and informs you that she was driven to an abortion clinic earlier that day, where her child was aborted. She is only 13. You didn't even know she was pregnant. She tells the story of how a few months ago, when she was 12 years old, the 18-year-old man she had been seeing—the man you tried to keep her from—had given her alcohol, gotten her drunk and impregnated her. The man's stepmother, upon learning her stepson had impregnated the girl, helped to arrange a plan to take your daughter, to drive her to another state and to abort her unborn child—all without informing you. Parents might think this was some sort of bad dream. But this nightmare happened in Pennsylvania—to Mrs. Joyce Farley and her daughter—and it has happened to other parents across the country.

How could this happen? In Pennsylvania, it is against the law to provide an abortion to a minor child without the consent of her parent, legal guardian, or a judge. But, in neighboring states like New York, it is not. The stepmother of that 18-year-old man, Ms. Rosa Marie Hartford, was later convicted of interference with the custody of children and sentenced to one year probation, 150 hours of community service and a $500 fine. Her lawyers appealed, challenging

Excerpted from Mike Fisher, *Child Custody Protection Act: Hearings on S. 1645*, 105th Congress, 2nd session, testimony before the U.S. Senate Committee on the Judiciary, May 20, 1998.

the constitutionality of the statute.

At the request of the county district attorney, my office stepped in to prosecute the appeal and defend the conviction. Although the Superior Court of Pennsylvania upheld the constitutionality of the statute, the case was remanded for a new trial because of an asserted error in the judge's instructions to the jury.

It is my understanding that this tragic case—*Commonwealth v. Rosa Marie Hartford* was part of the impetus for the introduction of the Child Custody Protection Act, or S. 1645. In many respects, that case underscores the necessity of this legislation.

Pennsylvania, as you know, has a strict parental consent/judicial bypass provision before a child under 18 years of age may lawfully obtain an abortion. New York, on the other hand, has no such requirement. A recitation of the facts in Hartford's case . . . demonstrate the need for passage of S. 1645.

A Missing Daughter

On August 31, 1995, Crystal Lane was enrolled at Sullivan County High School. She had turned 13 on July 20, 1995. Crystal was in eighth grade. She lived at home with her mother, Joyce Farley, her mother's fiancé, and her sister, Lisa. Crystal's parents were divorced. Pursuant to the divorce decree, Ms. Farley had custody of Crystal.

Crystal left the family residence early in the morning of August 31, 1995, before her mother awoke. She left her mother a note. Receiving a note of this sort was, according to Ms. Farley, "very odd" for Crystal. At that point, Crystal's mother began to search for her.

In addition to looking for Crystal herself, Ms. Farley called the high school and the Pennsylvania State Police. She called the state police because she was "very concerned" that Crystal was not at school. Ms. Farley was distraught over not knowing where Crystal was.

Later in the morning of August 31, 1995, Ms. Farley spoke with Lisa Cox, the mother of Crystal's friend, Alana Dangle. Upon speaking with Ms. Cox, Ms. Farley learned, for the first time, "that supposedly Crystal and Alana had gone to . . . New York or New Jersey for an abortion with a woman named Rosa." Before August 31, 1995, Ms. Farley did not even know that her 13-year-old daughter was pregnant. Ms. Farley did not give Crystal permission to be absent from

> *"[Imagine your daughter] informs you that she was driven to an abortion clinic . . . where her child was aborted. . . . You didn't even know she was pregnant."*

school or to travel anywhere on August 31, 1995. She did not give anyone permission to take Crystal anywhere on that date.

Before August 31, 1995, Ms. Farley had never met Rosa Hartford. She knew Hartford's son, Michael Kilmer. She had seen Kilmer with Crystal on a couple of occasions and told Crystal that Kilmer was too old for her and that she did not want him to come around their house. Kilmer was 18 at the time. She told Kilmer the same thing and not to call anymore. . . .

Nonetheless, during the summer of 1995, Crystal dated Kilmer, had sex with him, and became pregnant. Crystal realized she was pregnant in early to mid-August, within a month of her thirteenth birthday. She was then two months pregnant. She told her sister, Lisa (who was then fourteen or fifteen), Lisa's boyfriend, Craig Dostick, her friends, Alana Dangle and Erin Finch, and Michael Kilmer that she was pregnant. Crystal discussed her options with Kilmer, including the possibility of an abortion. Kilmer said he would pay for the abortion. Crystal also spoke with Hartford about the situation a few days before August 31, 1995.

Travel Plans

Melissa Hartford, Hartford's stepdaughter and Mike Kilmer's stepsister, called Crystal and provided her with information about where she could get an abortion. They discussed Melissa making an appointment for Crystal at Dr. Epstein's abortion clinic in New York. Melissa made the appointment in the name of "Crystal Hartford." It was planned that Kilmer would provide the money for the abortion. Melissa offered to drive Crystal to and from the abortion clinic.

On August 31, 1995, Crystal went to New York with Alana, Paul "Butch" Kemp, and Hartford. She left home at around 6:30 A.M. and was picked up at a prearranged location by Kent Hartford, Hartford's stepson. Either

> *"The states are constitutionally permitted to restrict the abortion rights of minors."*

Hartford or her stepdaughter, Melissa Hartford, had previously told her where to meet Kent. After Kent picked Crystal up they went to Alana's house to get her. From there they drove to Hartford's house. Hartford then drove Crystal and Alana to Paul "Butch" Kemp's house. Kemp drove all four to New York. Before that morning, Crystal thought that Melissa was driving her to New York. It was only that morning that she realized that Hartford was going to take her to the abortion clinic.

Though she knew before August 31, 1995, that Crystal was going to have an abortion, Hartford never asked Crystal if her mother knew of her situation. Hartford learned that Crystal was pregnant in early August when she overheard a friend of Michael Kilmer's ask Kilmer if he had yet told his family that Crystal was pregnant. The friend urged Kilmer to tell his family of Crystal's situation. Later Kilmer told Hartford that Crystal was pregnant and that he might be the father. Hartford knew that Kilmer had had sexual relations with Crystal. Kilmer gave Hartford the money for Crystal's abortion. Hartford even admitted to the police that it was possible that Kilmer was the father of Crystal's child.

Hartford was aware of the plans for Crystal to travel to New York for an abortion before August 31, 1995. A couple of days before August 31, 1995, Hartford and her daughter, Melissa, called Paul "Butch" Kemp to see if they could borrow his car so that Hartford could take two of her son's friends to a clinic in New York. On August 31, 1995, Hartford arrived at Mr. Kemp's house along with Crystal and Alana. and asked him to drive them to New York. He agreed. During the ride, Mr. Kemp learned he was going to an

> *"Parents [should] have a say in their child's decision whether to have an abortion."*

abortion clinic. When he learned that Crystal was pregnant and that she was being taken to the clinic for an abortion Mr. Kemp "felt like getting out." The trip to Binghamton took approximately one hour and forty-five minutes. They returned from New York at approximately 5:30 P.M.

Hartford's Deception

Hartford helped Crystal at the clinic. Crystal gave her last name as "Hartford" so the people at the abortion clinic would think she was Hartford's stepdaughter. Crystal signed a document at the clinic "Crystal Hartford." Hartford told the people at the clinic that she was Crystal's stepmother and signed a document to that effect. Crystal's abortion was paid for by Hartford with money she received for that purpose from her son, Michael Kilmer.

While at the abortion clinic, Hartford received a telephone call from her stepdaughter, Melissa. She advised Hartford that Crystal's mother had found out that Crystal had gone to New York to have an abortion and that Crystal's mother had called the state police. At that point, Hartford told the people at the abortion clinic that she was not Crystal's stepmother and that Crystal's real name was "Crystal Lane." This occurred after Crystal had already had the abortion. After hearing from Melissa, Hartford told Crystal that her mother knew that she had gone to Binghamton, New York, to have an abortion and that her mother had called the police.

On September 4, 1995, several days after she had taken her son's minor girlfriend to New York to have an abortion, Hartford called the abortion clinic and asked the receptionist to remove her name as Crystal's stepmother from the medical record. She made this request because the police had become involved in this matter.

On these facts Hartford was convicted of violating Pennsylvania's interference with custody of children statute which provides, in pertinent part: "A person commits an offense if he knowingly or recklessly takes or entices any child under the age of 18 years from the custody of its parent . . . when he has no privilege to do so." This statute, like S. 1645, "is intended to protect parental custody from unlawful interruption, even when the child is a willing participant in the interference with custody." Even so, the judges of the Superior Court, despite the fact that the issue was not before them, opined that this evidence was insufficient to sustain Hartford's conviction. This is perhaps the first reason why we need the "Child Custody Protection Act." It would clearly proscribe the conduct at issue in Hartford's case. . . .

Necessary Legislation

The *Hartford* case demonstrates the difficulties which states such as Pennsylvania encounter in trying to enforce their duly enacted laws. The states are constitutionally permitted to restrict the abortion rights of minors. As established in *Casey,* "a State may require a minor seeking an abortion to obtain the consent of a parent . . . provided there is an adequate judicial bypass procedure." As the Supreme Court noted in *H.L. v. Matheson* (1981): "Abortion is associated with an increased risk of complication in subsequent pregnancies. The emotional and psychological effects of the pregnancy and abortion experience are markedly more severe in girls under 18 than in adults."

Hopefully, S. 1645 will deter people like Rosa Hartford from transporting young girls across state lines to avoid abortion control acts like Pennsylvania's. Indeed, this kind of criminal behavior must not be tolerated. That is why I support the Child Custody Protection Act. This legislation will help us in law enforcement protect vulnerable children, by ensuring that parents have a say in their child's decision whether to have an abortion.

This legislation . . . will make it clear that a pregnant girl does not have a constitutional right to travel interstate to get an abortion; this will allow states to enforce their valid restrictions on abortion. Second, S. 1645 will make it clear that prohibiting an adult from taking a minor across state lines to obtain an abortion is not a burden on the right to interstate commerce. In America today, a 13-year-old girl cannot see the popular teenage movie *Scream* without the consent of her parents. She cannot get an aspirin from the school nurse, go on a class trip to the zoo or get her ear pierced without the consent of her parents. That same 13-year-old girl should at least be required to obtain the consent of her parents to get an abortion.

Had S. 1645 been in effect when the Farley family was victimized, law enforcement would have had an additional tool to ensure that parents have a say in this most personal, yet life-altering decision. That someone would take a 13-year-old girl away from her mother and, without her mother's knowledge or consent, drive the vulnerable girl to another state to abort her unborn child is a shocking violation of parental rights. Such actions should shock the conscience of any American.

We must do what we can to ensure that a parent's right to be involved in their daughter's decision regarding abortion is protected. I will continue to protect the rights of parents throughout Pennsylvania by defending our state parental consent law. I hope you will act to protect the rights of parents across this nation, by ensuring that strangers like Hartford are not allowed to violate the legal and emotional bond between a parent and a child.

Chapter 3

Should Women Have Greater Access to Abortion?

Chapter Preface

Ever since abortion was legalized by the Supreme Court in 1973 in its landmark decision *Roe v. Wade*, abortion opponents have tried to restrict the procedure or overturn the ruling. In the late 1990s, abortion opponents focused on the medical procedure known as intact dilation and extraction, more commonly called late-term or partial-birth abortion. The controversial procedure is used during the second or third trimester of a pregnancy and involves partially delivering the fetus in order to perform the abortion. Since 1995 opponents of late-term abortions have introduced bills in Congress to ban the procedure, but none has yet been passed into law.

Planned Parenthood and other pro-choice supporters contend that efforts to ban late-term abortions are thinly disguised attempts to ban abortion altogether. The legislation is so broad, its critics assert, that it could apply to abortion at any stage of pregnancy, not just the second or third trimester. According to Linda Gordon, a historian of gender and social policy at the University of Wisconsin, "Legislating at the state and federal level against 'partial-birth' abortion is the cutting-edge strategy in the drive to criminalize all abortion." Moreover, pro-choice sympathizers argue that late-term abortion is an extremely rare procedure; 99 percent of all abortions are performed in the first half of pregnancy, they assert, and less than 1 percent are performed after twenty-one weeks. In addition, they maintain that the vast majority of late-term abortions are the result of medical emergencies involving the health of the mother or the fetus.

Abortion opponents argue, however, that the procedure is cruel and should be banned. Ralph Reed, the former executive director of the Christian Coalition, asserts, "Partial-birth abortion is a never-necessary, health-threatening procedure for women that results in a painful and inhumane death for unborn babies." He and other members of the pro-life movement insist that late-term abortions are performed much more often than pro-choicers admit—and not just for medical emergencies. In addition to the procedure's overuse, its critics also complain that it can endanger a woman's health and future fertility.

The attempt to prohibit late-term abortion has generated much controversy among the pro-choice and pro-life movements. In the following chapter, the authors debate this heated topic and others while considering whether women should have greater access to abortion.

Women Need Greater Access to Abortion

by Marlene Gerber Fried

About the author: *Marlene Gerber Fried is a professor in the Civil Liberties and Public Policy Program at Hampshire College in Amherst, Massachusetts, and co-chair of the National Network of Abortion Funds.*

"Mary" calls me from South Dakota, asking if we can help. "Susan," her seventeen-year-old daughter, is pregnant. The man involved is the father of Susan's two-year-old child, but Susan has a restraining order against him. She is in her second trimester, and the only clinic in their state doesn't do abortions past fourteen weeks, so she will have to go to Kansas to have the abortion. Susan and her mother have tried, but they can't raise all the money needed for the trip and the procedure. The man's mother could contribute, but she is pressuring Susan to have the baby and give it to her to raise. Mary is worried and scared. She is also angry, after calling all the pro-choice groups she knows and finding no resources for women in her daughter's situation.

As the contact person for the National Network of Abortion Funds, I get many calls like this from women all over the country—women in prison, young women, women who have been raped, "undocumented" women, women without resources, desperate women. We repeatedly hear desperate stories from girls and women. A seventeen-year-old with one child, for example, drank a bottle of rubbing alcohol to cause a miscarriage; a fourteen-year-old asked her boyfriend to kick her in the stomach and push her down the stairs.

Although legal abortion is one of the safest surgical procedures in the United States—comparable to a tonsillectomy—these calls from low-income women are a constant reminder that safety itself is a privilege. Today, because of the inaccessibility of safe, legal abortion, some women are again resorting to illegal abortions and self-abortions. . . .

In the late 1990s the life of a woman who needs an abortion is most visibly endangered by the threat of personal violence. But even before she goes to a

Excerpted from Marlene Gerber Fried, "Abortion in the United States—Legal but Inaccessible," in *Abortion Wars: A Half Century of Struggle, 1950–2000*, edited by Rickie Solinger. Reprinted with permission from the University of California Press.

clinic, she may be endangered because she cannot find either a provider or the funds required. For women like Mary's daughter, it is as if *Roe v. Wade* never happened. And there are so many women like her, whose youth, race, and economic circumstances, together with the lack of accessible services—especially for later abortions—translate into daunting barriers. Before legalization, access to abortion was dependent on one's economic resources. Activists in the 1970s and 1980s who focused on the plight of low-income women saw that although legalization had tremendously increased accessibility, access was still dependent on ability to pay. In 1995 obstacles *define* abortion rights. The ability of a woman today to obtain an abortion is as dependent as ever on her economic status, age, race, and where she lives.

> *"Today, because of the inaccessibility of safe, legal abortion, some women are again resorting to illegal abortions and self-abortions."*

Since legalization of abortion in 1973, the anti-abortion movement has been pursuing a dual strategy, aiming at recriminalization of abortion in the long run while working to decrease access immediately. They have been successful. The abortion rights of uncountable women have effectively been taken away through the lack of federal and state funding, through decreases in available services and providers, by ongoing violence and harassment of clinics and clinic personnel, and by state legislative restrictions, such as parental consent laws and mandatory waiting periods. It is conservatively estimated that one in five Medicaid-eligible women wanting an abortion is unable to obtain it. This proportion will increase as women's economic situation worsens, as welfare is cut, as Medicaid is restricted (in 1995 Congress yielded to the religious right and permitted states to deny Medicaid funding for rape and incest), and as the anti-abortion movement moves on to new ground, as in the effort to outlaw certain late-term abortions.

The Battle Is Not Over

Although these erosions have shaped women's abortion experiences, many people, even those who favor abortion rights, are unaware of the realities of diminishing access. There is a widespread perception that the abortion battle is essentially over for now, with only the zealots on both sides still having the energy to fight. Articulating this view, a progressive woman columnist recently asked: Why the fuss about Charles Fried's nomination to the state supreme court in Massachusetts? Pro-choice activists found the question outrageous, given the candidate's background. When Fried served as solicitor general under Ronald Reagan, he aggressively worked against abortion rights. He argued to overturn *Roe v. Wade,* and after his government tenure he supported the "gag rule" preventing federally funded clinics from giving information about abortion. The columnist apparently thought this was irrelevant since, as she pointed out, the battle over abortion is over and the pro-choice side won. But has it?

The pro-choice movement itself has not adequately attended to access issues. Its focus has too often been on maintaining the legal right to abortion, while the unequal ability of different groups of women to exercise that right is slighted. The mainstream and predominantly white middle-class pro-choice movement has always responded weakly, if at all, to restrictions on low-income women's abortion rights. It was only in the 1980s, when *all* women's rights were threatened, that hundreds of thousands of women leaped to defend abortion clinics and *Roe v. Wade.* There have been no comparable large-scale mobilizations to protect the rights of low-income women. The challenge to the movement has been clearly stated by Joan Coombs, director of Planned Parenthood, Philadelphia: "Will women of means fight and be activists with and on behalf of poor women and teens just as if their own rights were under attack?"

Thus far, the answer has been no. . . .

A Need for Federal Funding

The impact of eroding access to abortion has been felt most severely by low-income women, young women, and women of color, who comprise a disproportionate number of the poor. Access has been undermined primarily through denial of public funding for abortion, parental involvement laws, and the loss of abortion services.

Public funding, an absolute necessity if all women are to have access to abortion rights, was lost in *1976,* just three years after *Roe v. Wade.* The Hyde Amendment, which prohibits federal Medicaid funding except in cases of life endangerment, has been renewed by Congress every year since. Most states have followed the federal precedent and prohibit the use

> *"The impact of eroding access to abortion has been felt most severely by low-income women, young women, and women of color."*

of state funds for abortions. As of September 1995, only 13 percent of abortions were paid for with public funds, almost all state funds; and as of January 1996, only seventeen states covered abortions for health reasons.

Exceptions for rape and incest were added to Hyde in 1993, only after a long battle. Even this minimal "liberalization" was resisted, and several states refused to comply. In August 1995 Congress rescinded the exceptions and returned to life endangerment as the only grounds for funding.

Virtually No Women Qualify for Support

Between 1973 and 1977 the federal government paid for about one-third of all abortions: 294,600 in 1977. After Hyde the decline was dramatic, and it continued over the following decade. In 1978 fewer than 2,500 abortions were covered by federal Medicaid funds (down 99 percent from 1977). By 1992 Medicaid paid for only 267 abortions. A few examples illustrate how the rigid federal standard has disqualified virtually all women from federal support.

- A twenty-three-year-old woman with cervical cancer was told that Medicaid would pay for a hysterectomy but not for an abortion, which was a prerequisite to appropriate treatment of the disease.
- A woman who had tried to self-abort with a coat hanger was hospitalized with an infection. Medicaid paid for treating the infection but would not pay for an abortion because her pregnancy was not seen as life-threatening.
- A woman carrying a twenty-two-week fetus with a fatal heart defect was denied funding for an abortion.

The Hyde Amendment primarily affects low-income women, but it also applies to federal workers, military personnel and their dependents, women living on Native American reservations, and women in federal prisons. Its impact has been devastating. The average cost of a first-trimester abortion is $296, nearly two-thirds the amount of the average maximum monthly payment under Aid to Families with Dependent Children (AFDC) for a family of three. Clearly, some welfare recipients cannot afford abortions at all. Others are forced to divert money from other essentials, such as food, rent, and utilities. Even when women are able to raise the money, the time it takes to search for funding makes it more likely they will need a more costly and more difficult second-trimester procedure. It is estimated that one in five Medicaid-eligible women who had second-trimester abortions would have had a first-trimester abortion if the lack of public funds had not resulted in delays while the woman was trying to raise funds.

A Shortage of Abortion Providers

The lack of funding contributes to other aspects of diminished access, including the unavailability of abortion services and the decrease in the number of abortion providers. Significantly fewer hospitals, clinics, and private physicians' offices provide abortions in states with funding restrictions.

Publicity surrounding the murders of doctors and clinic workers has made the public at large sharply aware of the extreme vulnerability of abortion providers.

"Few medical students are being trained in abortion techniques, despite the fact that abortion is the most common obstetrics surgical procedure."

In fact, clinics and providers have been targets of violence since the early 1980s. In 1993 alone, half of all clinics responding to a survey about clinic violence reported severe anti-abortion attacks. These acts included death threats, stalking, attacks with chemicals such as butyric acid, arson, bomb threats, invasions, and blockades. While federal legislation such as the Freedom of Access to Clinic Entrances (FACE) Act will certainly help, anti-abortionists are increasingly turning to harassment of individual doctors and their families, picketing their homes, following them, circulating "Wanted" posters.

The provider shortage has only recently come to public attention, although it represents a major threat to abortion rights. The number of abortion providers (including hospitals, clinics, and physicians' offices) dropped 18 percent between 1982 and 1992, with the greatest loss occurring between 1988 and 1992.

"One-quarter of women having abortions travel more than fifty miles from home to obtain their abortions."

While the overall numbers themselves are very disturbing, of even greater concern is the very uneven distribution of services. Nine of ten abortion providers are now located in metropolitan areas; about one-third fewer counties have an abortion provider now than did in the late 1970s. Ninety-four percent of nonmetropolitan counties have no services (85 percent of rural women live in these underserved counties). One-quarter of women having abortions travel more than fifty miles from home to obtain their abortions.

Anti-abortion activists aim also to cut off the supply of potential future providers. They have targeted medical students, generating understandable concerns about taking up practice in such a dangerous and marginalized field. A group called Life Dynamics promoted its agenda with "Bottom Feeder," a fourteen-page "joke" book sent to 35,000 medical students. One of the jokes: "What do you do if you find yourself in a room with Hitler, Mussolini and an abortionist, and you have only two bullets? *Answer:* Shoot the abortionist twice." Each person receiving the mailing is also told: "The anti-abortion movement knows where to find you."

Few medical students are being trained in abortion techniques, despite the fact that abortion is the most common obstetrics surgical procedure. Almost half of graduating obstetrics and gynecology residents have never performed a first-trimester abortion. Many hospitals do so few abortions they cannot even be appropriate training sites. In February 1995 the American Council for Graduate Medical Education issued guidelines mandating abortion training. Anti-abortion challenges were immediately set in motion, and by August 1995 Congress had voted to protect federal funds for medical schools that refuse to teach abortion techniques. . . .

All of these infringements on abortion access have curtailed the abortion rights of millions of women. In addition, the anti-abortion movement has used access issues to further its long-term political objective of criminalizing abortion. Anti-abortion activists have been able to use battles over funding, training of doctors, and parental consent as opportunities for consolidating their movement, drawing in new supporters, and building support for other restrictions on abortion.

The RU-486 Abortion Pill Should Be Available to Women

by Laura Fraser

About the author: *Journalist Laura Fraser writes the Well-Being column for* Mother Jones.

Anti-abortion protesters, gun-shy drug companies, and timid politicians have stymied RU 486 for a decade. . . .

In 1988, *Mother Jones* announced a "birth control breakthrough" on its cover, describing the development of a promising new "abortion pill"—RU 486—and asking why, if it worked so well for French, Chinese, Swedish, and Dutch women, it wasn't available in the United States. The physicians, feminists, and family-planning experts I interviewed then predicted that, given the political climate surrounding abortion, it could be 10 years before RU 486, or mifepristone, would be approved for use by American women.

Eleven years later, U.S. doctors still can't prescribe the drug. But if all goes smoothly, they may get to sometime in [the future]. The FDA has given mifepristone preliminary approval, and, equally significant, manufacturers have been identified. Don't hold your breath, though: Formidable political obstacles have long kept mifepristone from pharmacy shelves, and plenty more could arise.

Improving Access to Abortion

If and when mifepristone does become available, it will remove many of the political and practical barriers that have made it difficult for U.S. women to get abortions—and for many physicians to perform them. A survey of physicians conducted by the Kaiser Family Foundation and published in September 1998 found that 54 percent of all obstetricians and gynecologists, including 45 percent of those who don't currently perform abortions, said they would offer mifepristone if it were available.

The greatest victory of the anti-abortion movement has been to move a straightforward procedure out of the medical schools, out of the hospitals, and into freestanding, sitting-duck clinics. Mifepristone's promise is that it can bring abortion back into the mainstream and into the hands of the family physician or small-town gynecologist. In a country where 86 percent of counties have no known abortion providers, there's no doubt mifepristone would make abortion more accessible. "We're talking about expanding the pool of providers from literally a handful to many, many, many," says Eric Schaff, an associate professor at the University of Rochester, who is conducting clinical trials of mifepristone.

It isn't as if mifepristone will completely defuse the abortion controversy. Even if the drug is approved, many women will still need surgical abortions. Mifepristone works early by blocking the hormone progesterone from reaching uterine cell receptors. Without progesterone, the uterine lining can't grow and nourish the fertilized egg, which then detaches. A day or two later, women take a second drug, misoprostol, a prostaglandin that causes the uterus to contract, expelling its contents as in a normal menstrual period. The procedure works best within seven weeks of the woman's last period. In the United States, more than half of all abortions—or 736,000 per year—are performed by nine weeks, according to the Alan Guttmacher Institute, which tracks abortion statistics. It isn't clear how many of these women would choose a medical abortion over a surgical one—but one can guess. "All we know," says Heather O'Neill of the Danco Group, which is seeking to market the drug, "is that, given the option, one-third of French women chose to have a medical abortion."

Women who have tried mifepristone have been satisfied with the results, saying they find it less physically and emotionally invasive than surgery. Ninety-six percent of women in one U.S. clinical trial said they'd recommend the medication to others who needed an abortion, according to a study published in the *Archives of Family Medicine.* Of the women who had also experienced a surgical abortion, three-quarters preferred the drug. Even among women for whom the drug failed (8 percent at the seven-week mark in one clinical trial), 70 percent said they'd try it again if needed. The procedure isn't without side effects—including nausea, vomiting, headaches, and diarrhea—but it is remarkably safe. Among the estimated 2 million women who have used mifepristone worldwide, there has been only one reported death, and that was due to a type of prostaglandin no longer in use, not mifepristone. Currently, an estimated 80,000 women die annually from botched abortions around the globe.

> *"Mifepristone's promise is that it can bring abortion back into the mainstream."*

Once approved, mifepristone will likely have many other uses. Numerous studies have proved it safe and effective, and have suggested it may be helpful in treating other women's health concerns, such as endometriosis, fibroid tumors, difficult labors, and a type of brain tumor. Most of those studies have stopped as researchers have run out of the drug, but will continue once it's available again.

Anti-Abortion Barricades

Despite mifepristone's likely popularity, the anti-abortion movement has succeeded in keeping it off the U.S. market. Since 1982, when researchers for the French company Roussel Uclaf reported that the drug could terminate pregnancy, abortion foes have worked on several fronts to stop it. In 1988, when the French minister of health approved the general use of the drug, opponents assailed RU 486 as a "chemical weapon" against the unborn. They organized protest marches through Paris and temporarily succeeded in getting Roussel to withdraw the pill from the market. The French government, which owned 36 percent of Roussel, muscled it back (hailing it as the "moral property of women"), but Hoechst, the company's parent—which had about $7 billion in annual pharmaceutical sales in the United States and a devout Catholic president—was daunted by the possibility of similar boycotts here.

> *"Despite mifepristone's likely popularity, the anti-abortion movement has succeeded in keeping it off the U.S. market."*

Feminist groups, particularly the Feminist Majority Foundation, lobbied Roussel to bring RU 486 to the United States, but to no avail. In 1990, the American Medical Association argued that the drug should be made available in the United States on the grounds that an equally effective noninvasive procedure is always preferable to a surgical one. Conservative Republicans, however, kept pressure on the Bush administration to ban the drug's introduction.

With Bill Clinton in office, things began to give. In 1993, Clinton issued an executive memorandum to Health and Human Services Secretary Donna Shalala to investigate possibilities for bringing mifepristone into this country. Then, in 1994, Roussel Uclaf donated the U.S. patent rights for mifepristone to the Population Council, a nonprofit research group, which promptly began a clinical trial. In 1996, reviewing the data, the FDA issued qualified approval of the drug, pending information on labeling and manufacturing.

But finding a manufacturer has also proved difficult. Pharmaceutical companies were largely unwilling to take on a relatively small-revenue drug that carries a high risk of political fallout—and not just from anti-abortion protesters. Several mutual funds with anti-abortion agendas have said they will exclude manufacturers of mifepristone from their portfolios. "If we invest in companies," says Frank Rauscher, CEO of the Aquinas Funds, "we want to make sure the companies are involved in ethical and legitimate activities." He adds that Merck, Johnson & Johnson, Schering-Plough, Pharmacia & Upjohn, and Pfizer have all told him they will not manufacture the drug.

Last year, the Population Council licensed the Danco Group to market mifepristone. Danco has, at long last, found manufacturers—which it would not identify—willing to do the job. "We expect to make [mifepristone] available to women in the U.S. sometime in 1999," says the Danco Group's O'Neill.

Regardless of when the drug is approved, the trend toward earlier, more accessible abortions seems clear. Several Planned Parenthood clinics now offer abortions induced with methotrexate—a cancer drug that works more slowly than mifepristone and is not approved by the FDA as an abortifacient. Also, more physicians are offering earlier, less invasive surgical abortions, using manual suction techniques and a syringe instead of a machine vacuum. "Regardless of how soon mifepristone becomes available," says Paul Blumenthal, medical director for Planned Parenthood of Maryland, "women will have more choices for terminating an unwanted pregnancy."

Late-Term Abortions Should Not Be Banned

by Gloria Feldt

About the author: *Gloria Feldt is president of the Planned Parenthood Federation of America.*

Claudia Crown Ades discovered in her 26th week of pregnancy that the baby she desperately wanted was doomed by extensive damage to the brain, heart, and internal organs.

Mary-Dorothy Line learned at 19 weeks that there was no hope for her pregnancy. The skull of her fetus had filled with fluid in place of a developed brain.

And then there's Vikki Stella. In her 32nd week of pregnancy, an ultrasound determined that something was terribly wrong. Testing ultimately confirmed nine major anomalies, including a fluid-filled cranium with no brain tissue at all. A diabetic, Vikki could not have continued the pregnancy without endangering her health, due to increased risk of blood loss during delivery.

These women—all in their 20s and 30s—were advised by their physicians that the abortion procedure called intact D&E [dilation and extraction] was the best option to terminate their pregnancies safely, without endangering their future fertility.

Today, these women are healthy, and Mary-Dorothy and Vikki have since given birth to healthy babies. Why? They were able to make a choice. In a similar situation, it's a choice you won't have if some members of Congress have their way. . . .

Congress [continues to consider] legislation that would ban so-called partial-birth abortions—a vague and medically inaccurate term. The bill's language is so broad that the procedure which protected the health of Vikki and the others would be only one of many methods banned. Circumstances can and do arise during standard D&E and induced-delivery abortions that would place these common procedures and nearly all other abortion procedures within the bill's definition of "partial-birth" abortion.

If passed, the bill would mark the first time Congress has ever outlawed a

Reprinted from Gloria Feldt, "The Abortion Debate," *Cosmopolitan*, July 1997. Reprinted with permission from Planned Parenthood Federation of America.

specific medical procedure. This would endanger women's health, overrule the best judgment of physicians, and set a dangerous precedent for government intrusion into private medical decisions.

Understanding those dangers means getting past the confusion created by the bill's supporters—extremists who oppose all abortions at any stage of pregnancy for any reason. Their strategy, Ralph Reed [former head of the Christian Coalition] told the *New York Times,* is to outlaw abortion one procedure at a time, starting with this bill.

The Supreme Court decided in 1973 in the case of *Roe v. Wade* that before viability (roughly the first 24 weeks of a normal 40-week pregnancy), the circumstances of a woman's abortion decision should not be judged by anyone.

Abortions after the point of viability are exceedingly rare. The Alan Guttmacher Institute estimates that 320 to 600 are performed after the 26th week in the entire country each year and only in cases of severe fetal anomaly or threat to the woman's life and health.

But the issue isn't about numbers. It's about the health and lives of women, which are being callously disregarded by those determined to pass this misguided bill.

If Congress wants to reduce abortions in the later stages of pregnancy, it should take stronger action to prevent harassment of women at health centers (angry picketers, bombings), which causes some women to delay their abortion decision. Parental-consent requirements and mandatory waiting periods are also burdensome obstacles to the young and poor. And Congress should ensure access to medical abortions, such as those that use mifepristone and methotrexate.

What Congress should not do is pass a law that implies that women make these difficult life decisions on a whim. For every fiction that anti-abortion groups concoct—that women seek abortions for reasons as trivial as wanting to fit into their prom dress—there is a woman like Vikki or Claudia or Mary-Dorothy who faces a terrible reality.

> *"This [ban] would endanger women's health . . . and set a dangerous precedent for government intrusion into private medical decisions."*

In the 27 years since *Roe,* American women have not had one moment's rest—not from legislative attempts to restrict their rights to abortion nor from violent protesters willing to use any means to interfere with a woman's private and personal decision including the harassment and assassination of women's reproductive health providers. I am still amazed by those who would look into the eyes of a woman in crisis and say, "We're not doctors and we're not your family, but we'll decide what you can or cannot do."

Women Have Sufficient Access to Abortion

by David Whitman

About the author: *David Whitman is a senior writer for* U.S. News & World Report.

For a fleeting moment in October 1998, Michelle Lee became the emblem of the abortion-rights movement. The 26-year-old divorced mother of two suffered from a life-threatening heart condition. Her heart was so fragile that Louisiana State University Medical Center in Shreveport had put her on the transplant list and her cardiologist had warned that another pregnancy could kill her. Yet when she unexpectedly became pregnant last summer, the LSU Medical Center refused to give her an abortion. The reason: A panel of the state hospital's physicians concluded that Lee's chances of dying from her pregnancy were less than 50 percent.

The hospital's decision prompted [journalist] Connie Chung to pointedly ask on *Good Morning America* whether "the hospital [was] willing to let her die." Within days, the National Abortion Federation (NAF) raised $7,000 to pay for Lee's abortion, found an obstetrician and hospital in Houston to perform the procedure, and had a medic unit drive her 240 miles to the hospital. Lee later returned quietly to Bossier City—where, only weeks later, she had another heart attack.

For abortion-rights advocates, Michelle Lee is Exhibit A that the right to abortion is endangered, even in cases where a woman's life is plainly at risk. Ironically, though, antiabortion activists also hold up Lee as proof that the right to abortion remains intact. "What did it take her—all of a week to find an abortion?" scoffs Sandy McDade, the chairperson of the Eagle Forum of Louisiana. It took longer than a week, but McDade has a point. Statistics show a sharp and ongoing drop in the number of abortion providers since 1982. But despite all the new state restrictions and a perceived climate of violent protests, there's little evidence that women who want abortions today can't get them. The largely

Excerpted from David Whitman, "Abortion: The Untold Story," *U.S. News & World Report*, December 7, 1998. Copyright ©1998 by *U.S. News & World Report*. Reprinted with permission.

untold story is that fewer women—including teens—are having abortions.

The abortion rate recently hit its lowest level since 1975. States reported 1.21 million abortions to the Centers for Disease Control and Prevention (CDC) in 1995, down from the CDC's peak tally of 1.43 million in 1990. Contrary to the arguments of some abortion-rights groups, however, the drop does not seem to stem from a decline in the accessibility of abortions. Rather, it appears that fewer women need them: Since 1990, birthrates have been going down, too, suggesting that women are not being forced to carry to term. Studies show that, prompted by the fear of AIDS, some teens are waiting longer to have sex, and more sexually active teenagers now use contraceptives than in the 1980s. What's more, despite the murder in October 1998 of Buffalo obstetrician Barnett Slepian, antiabortion violence is down from its peaks in 1992 and 1989.

Drive Time

Statistics . . . released December 11, 1998, by New York's Alan Guttmacher Institute—a reproductive health research center—show that as of 1996 (the most recent data available), the number of abortion facilities fell to their lowest total since 1974, a year after the Supreme Court legalized abortion. (In 1974, there were 2,004 abortion facilities.) By 1992, when there were 2,400 abortion facilities, 84 percent of U.S. counties did not have one. In addition, Congress has barred the use of federal Medicaid funds for routine abortions, 29 states now require minors to notify or get parental or judicial consent for an abortion, and arsons and bomb attacks on clinics are up since 1996.

Yet some purported examples of curtailed abortion access are less real than they seem. For instance, while it is true that 84 percent of counties lack abortion facilities, 70 percent of women of childbearing age lived in counties with facilities in 1992. The other 30 percent are concentrated in rural counties. Stories about long commutes in sparsely populated states like North Dakota have become news media staples, although only about 8 percent of the women who got abortions in 1992—the latest year for which stats are available—drove more than 100 miles, according to the Guttmacher Institute.

In the wake of Slepian's murder, abortion-rights activists have portrayed clinics as "war zones," as Kate Michelman, president of the National

> *"There's little evidence that women who want abortions today can't get them."*

Abortion and Reproductive Rights Action League, puts it. "They have armed guards, the doctors wear bulletproof vests, and women fear for their lives as they try to obtain abortion services," she says. But many abortion clinics are more like Hope Medical Group for Women in Shreveport, which has had scares but no injuries or death threats. The most serious incident occurred [in 1983], when a man wielding an oversized sledgehammer began smashing windows, doors, and walls after announcing he had been "sent by the Lord, and the building is coming down." Patients were evacuated, and no one was injured. Around the same time, bullets fired after-hours shattered the clinic's windows, which have since been boarded up. Over the years, the clinic has also had sporadic protests and was once blockaded. But Robin Rothrock, the clinic's administrator, says there haven't been any organized protests for two years.

No Choice

In upstate New York, not even a doctor's chilling murder has stopped the flow of patients. "I asked the women, 'Aren't you afraid?' and they said, 'Sure, but I have no other choice,'" says Melinda DuBois, assistant director of Buffalo GYN Womenservices, where Slepian performed abortions. The response isn't unusual. After police in Shreveport hauled away the man with the sledgehammer, every patient returned. "The women were saying, 'I want to be next,'" Rothrock recalls.

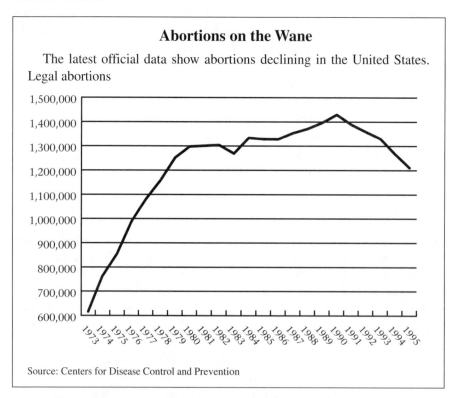

Abortions on the Wane

The latest official data show abortions declining in the United States. Legal abortions

Source: Centers for Disease Control and Prevention

[In 1998], the Bureau of Alcohol, Tobacco and Firearms . . . reported eight bombings and four arsons at the country's 2,000 or so abortion facilities. That means that more than 99 percent of the nation's facilities weren't hit. Arsons reported to the bureau peaked in 1992 when 21 fires were set; the most bombings—11—took place in 1984. A new federal law enacted in 1994, which created criminal penalties for obstructing, intimidating, or interfering with women seeking abortions, helped slash the number of clinic blockades from 201 in 1989 to 25 [in 1997]. Death threats are down, too, from 78 in 1993 to 11 in 1997, according to the National Abortion Federation (NAF), an umbrella group of abortion providers. And murders, while shocking, are rare. The first slaying at an abortion clinic, that of physician David Gunn in Pensacola, Fla., occurred in 1993. [In 1998]—after three years without any slayings—two U.S. abortion clinic workers were killed—Slepian and an off-duty police officer guarding an Alabama clinic.

While most types of antiabortion violence have ebbed over the years, disruptive tactics like picketing, hate mail, and bomb threats reached record highs in 1997. The most common tactic, by far, is picketing—NAF reported more than 7,500 incidents of picketing during 1997. Clinics in 21 of 43 states surveyed by NAF last year reported weekly or daily protests.

Proximity to clinics doesn't seem to be much of a deterrent. As abortion-rights advocates have long attested, women will go to great lengths—and distances—to get an abortion. Louisiana, which has some of the nation's most restrictive abortion laws, is a textbook example. The state has a 24-hour waiting period. During a patient's initial visit to a clinic, doctors detail the developmental stages of a fetus. Women also receive a state-sponsored booklet that illustrates fetal development from weeks 2 through 38, and a directory of abortion alternatives. Minors need a parent's—or judge's—notarized consent for an abortion. And abortion clinics are scarce—92 percent of the state's parishes have no provider.

"In upstate New York, not even a doctor's chilling murder has stopped the flow of patients."

But Louisiana's abortion providers help women navigate the restrictions. Hope Medical Group and another clinic across the Red River in Bossier City are the only abortion providers within a 150-mile radius of Shreveport. Hope has Saturday and Tuesday evening hours to accommodate working women and has a notary on staff to make it easier for teens—although many minors instead go to Texas, which doesn't require parental consent. Most women can pay the $245 for a first trimester abortion. But those who can't, pay in installments, and the clinic sometimes subsidizes the tab of those too poor to pay.

Hope—and other clinics—often tap the National Network of Abortion Funds (NNAF) for aid. The network includes 57 individual funds in 29 states. In 1997, it provided $1 million to help finance 15,000 abortions. NNAF member funds, for example, provided $5,600 toward Michelle Lee's abortion.

Getting Results

Rothrock and other abortion-rights advocates acknowledge they don't personally know of women who wanted—and were eligible for—an abortion but were denied one. Joyce Schorr, who heads the Women's Reproductive Rights Assistance Project, one of NNAF's affiliates, reports that over the past seven years her group has fully or partially funded 2,000 abortions. "Anytime we have taken a call [on our hot line], we helped that clinic take care of the woman," says Schorr, noting, however, that the hot line occasionally shuts down for lack of money. Maureen Britell, government relations director for the National Abortion Federation, says she lined up abortions for all but one of the 44 cases referred to her over the past six months. (The failed case involved an incest victim who was in her seventh month of pregnancy, too late for an abortion unless the mother's life or health is endangered.) It was Britell who found a doctor to perform Michelle Lee's abortion and who raised the funds to pay for it.

> *"At least since the late 1980s, poor and minority women don't appear to have less access."*

Abortion-choice activists believe some women don't get abortions because of the cost. But at least since the late 1980s, poor and minority women don't appear to have less access. While the total number of abortions has declined since 1985, the number of taxpayer-financed abortions has risen, from a minimum of 188,000 publicly funded abortions in 1985 to more than 203,000 such abortions in 1994. In 1995, nonwhites accounted for a larger share of all abortions (40.5 percent) than 10 years earlier (33.3 percent), according to the CDC.

The United States still has some of the highest rates of unplanned pregnancy and abortion in the industrialized world. Half of the nation's pregnancies are unintended, and, at current rates, 43 percent of American women will have at least one abortion before turning 45, according to the Guttmacher Institute.

President Clinton has set a goal that abortions be "safe, legal, and rare." Almost six years into his presidency, abortion is still safe, legal, and has declined modestly in numbers. No one, however, can say that it is rare.

The RU-486 Abortion Pill Should Not Be Available to Women

by Lawrence F. Roberge

About the author: *Lawrence F. Roberge is a biotechnology consultant, college instructor, bioethicist, and biomedical researcher. He is also the author of the book* The Cost of Abortion.

Is the emotional and political reaction to President Bill Clinton's 1996 veto of the partial birth abortion ban a surprise to anyone? Probably not. What is surprising is the scope of the emotional opposition to partial birth abortion as seen against the flimsy backdrop of political and social apathy that has been the norm during more than 24 years of legalized abortion in the United States.

Why such a reaction from pro-life and Church leaders now? Many of the same leaders never unleashed the same kind of fury or generated the same type of media coverage during the past 24 relentless years of abortion-on-demand. It's almost as though, in some people's minds, the horror of abortion becomes real only at advanced gestational age or by virtue of the physical location of the tiny victim at the time it's killed.

The availability of abortion clinics and doctors is slowly dwindling. Organized protests at clinics and doctors' homes, and the filing of malpractice suits against abortion doctors, have contributed to the decline in available abortion facilities and physicians. How will abortion continue as a method of eugenics and population control; as an erroneously described "reproductive right"? Perhaps the answers to these questions will yield clues to the future of abortion.

Technological Advances

As technology advances in the fields of endocrinology, biotechnology, immunology and pharmacology, the creation of new abortifacient technologies will continue. Furthermore, these technologies will target the destruction of life

Excerpted from Lawrence F. Roberge, "Killing by Caplet: Is Abortion Coming Home?" *Human Life International*, March 1997. Reprinted with permission from the author.

at an ever-earlier stage of development. The movement of technologies to destroy life will continue to focus at the embryonic (up to two months of development) state.

This statement is substantiated by U.S. Food and Drug Administration (FDA) approval of double-dose birth control pills and FDA market approval of RU-486 (mifepristone). The purpose of double-dose birth control pills is to block uterine implantation of an early stage embryo, whereas the progesterone blocking action of RU-486 acts to terminate embryonic life up to the first 49 days of development.

Beyond these approved drugs, the development of other embryonic stage abortifacients (such as more advanced progesterone blockers . . .) is continuing. Furthermore, the development of an abortifacient vaccine is nearly complete. This technology does not block ovulation or conception, but rather blocks embryo implantation and leads to embryonic death, which appears as a menstrual period. This technology is targeted for world distribution. The vaccines will mislead many to believe they are using a safe, effective form of birth control when, in reality, the vaccine will engineer a monthly abortion. The vaccine's effects will last for 18 months.

The destructive effect of many of these products that kill the embryo in early stages of development bring us to the next clue to the future of abortion.

Moving Away from Fetal Death

Advances in technology will reduce the fetal body count while vastly increasing embryonic fatalities. As a consequence, this may increase societal acceptance of abortion. How? Abortifacient technologies will destroy life at earlier stages. Market studies for RU-486 alone claim that product could capture up to 60% of the clinical surgical abortion market in the U.S. Other technologies could surpass that figure.

Furthermore, one method that pro-lifers use to convey the "humanness" of the unborn baby is to display graphic photos of fetuses with well-formed fingers, eyes, hands, toes, a heart beating, etc. Advanced abortifacient technologies act to destroy the life in the embryonic (e.g. trophoblastic) stage, well *before* toes, eyes, hands, etc. are formed. Also, it will be harder to emotionally associate with a "hollow ball of cells" (as in the case of the trophoblastic embryo) than with a human-shaped fetus. In essence, the myth that abortion just removes a "blob of cells or tissue" will be reinforced.

> *"[Abortifacient technologies will reinforce] the myth that abortion just removes a 'blob of cells or tissue.'"*

Even now, the beginning of life is being redefined at the uterine implantation stage (nidation), rather than at conception. This redefinition allows justification for such medical activities as human embryo experimentation and the recently publicized incident in Britain of the disposal of thousands of human embryos. This redefinition has been supported by the National Institutes of Health (NIH) and the American Fertility Society (AFS).

This new redefining of the pre-embryo as less than totally human life affords not merely research on human embryos, but expanded use of abortifacients that destroy early life by killing the pre-embryo or blocking uterine implantation. (Remember: blocking uterine implantation leads to rapid death of the embryo). At present, some forms of birth control (e.g., intrauterine devices [IUDs] and some versions of the birth control pills), already block embryonic implantation into the uterus.

> *"The population will increasingly be deceived into accepting abortifacients as a version of effective birth control."*

As more data arise on the complications due to surgically induced abortions, marketing strategies for abortifacient products will capitalize on this data as a motivational factor toward more embryo-stage directed abortifacients.

Simply put, pharmaceutical corporations will use available data on abortion complications (e.g., the abortion and infertility link; abortion and breast cancer link, etc.) to convince consumers to use birth control that in reality is abortifacient in nature. As the population of consumers accepting this technology increases, total surgical abortions will rapidly decrease, while the total number of abortions will rise exponentially. In reality, the population will increasingly be deceived into accepting abortifacients as a version of effective birth control.

The shift from surgical abortions to pharmaceutical abortifacients brings us to the next aspect of the future of abortion.

Abortifacients and the Pharmaceutical Industry

The market shift to pharmaceutical abortifacients has some advantages. First, this technology reduces the role of clinics and doctors. Doctors need not use a clinic to prescribe or dispense pharmaceutical abortifacients. Rather, doctors may dispense these drugs (or vaccines) in their office and such actions will be protected by doctor-patient confidentiality.

Also, as previously noted, increasing dissemination of pharmaceutical abortifacients will lead to a decrease in surgical abortions. As surgical abortions decrease, this will reduce abortion clinic revenues. Eventually, the declining revenues may force many clinics to close.

Although some clinics may continue to exist, by virtue of the need to distribute abortifacient drugs, the most cost effective measure for physicians (and health care providers like HMOs and PPOs) will be abortifacient distribution at the physician's office.

This shift in abortion (from surgical means to pharmaceuticals) will further favor the physician in another way.

One of the strong deterrents for physicians working in the abortion industry is malpractice suits. In recent years, a combined force of pro-life advocates and legal professionals have unleashed a torrent of malpractice suits due to botched abortions. As a result, physician malpractice suits and malpractice financial settlements have climbed.

As abortifacient technology favors pharmaceuticals, the resultant legal/financial responsibility shifts away from the sole physician toward the larger (and more legally formidable) pharmaceutical corporations. The costs of malpractice insurance would be comparably lower (by dispensing abortifacients) even though the physician's participation in abortion would continue.

Malpractice suits would be replaced by drug manufacturer lawsuits which are more lengthy, costly and more difficult to win. Furthermore, recent FDA bias toward RU-486 may require future lawsuits against this federal agency. Lawsuits at this level are even more lengthy and difficult (if not impossible) to win.

Making Abortion More Palatable

The distribution of abortifacients by doctors may make abortion more palatable to physicians. One case in point: A 1995 Kaiser Family Foundation survey has found that doctors who would not perform surgical abortions would prescribe the abortifacient drug, RU-486. Furthermore, the same survey demonstrated that a majority of the doctors who do not perform abortions have prescribed the "morning after pill" for emergency contraception. As more abortifacient products enter the marketplace, physicians (even with their knowledge base of endocrinology, pharmacology and gynecology—as well as the understanding of the consequences of the use of abortifacient drugs and vaccines)—will increasingly turn to prescribe these products to terminate early stage pregnancies.

Recently, Americans have enjoyed the no-prescription availability of commonly used pharmaceutical products like Nicorette gum, Tagament, Zantac, Rogaine, and Naproxin (aka Aleve). The process to move a prescription drug to over-the-counter drug status (commonly referred to as RX-to-OTC conversions) has been accelerating during this decade. Usually, the motivational factor for this conversion is the end of the pharmaceutical firm's exclusive marketing of this product as its patent expires.

"Should pro-life forces fail to warn society about the future of abortion and its implications . . . American society itself may eventually be faced with obsolescence."

At present, the only class of drugs for which the FDA will absolutely not allow RX-to-OTC conversions are narcotics. It is conceivable that eventually some abortifacient pharmaceuticals (as their patents come up to the expiration date) will become available over the counter. Women soon may be able to obtain abortifacients at their discount drugstores as easily as purchasing aspirin, antacids, panty hose or nail polish! . . .

The Future of Abortion

The future of abortion is a future which will involve technologies that destroy life at a much earlier stage of development. As such, chemical methods of killing babies will increase public acceptance of abortion, reduce the overall costs to pro-abortion facilities, reduce reproductive responsibility and mute much of the societal emotional response to those destroyed in the womb.

The response to the future of abortion is twofold. The challenge to pro-lifers will require the acquisition of scientific and technological staffers who can comprehend and educate the public on these technologies and their consequences. Furthermore, a re-examination of the connection between contraception and abortion is required.

Finally, should pro-life forces fail to warn society about the future of abortion and its implications—and should those warnings continue to be ignored—American society itself may eventually be faced with obsolescence.

Rationale for Banning Abortions Late in Pregnancy

by M. LeRoy Sprang and Mark G. Neerhof

About the authors: *M. LeRoy Sprang and Mark G. Neerhof are physicians in Illinois.*

The abortion issue remains in the public eye and the media headlines largely because of a single late-term abortion procedure referred to in the medical literature as intact dilation and extraction (D&X) and in the common vernacular as partial-birth abortion. This viewpoint reviews the medical and ethical aspects of this procedure and of late-term abortions in general.

Conflicting Information

Intact D&X came to the forefront of public awareness in 1995 during a congressional debate on a bill banning the procedure. During this debate, opponents of the ban asserted that the procedure was rarely performed (approximately 450–500 per year) and only used in extreme cases when a woman's life was at risk or the fetus had a condition incompatible with life. Following President Bill Clinton's April 1996 veto of a congressionally approved ban, conflicting information surfaced. Ron Fitzsimmons, executive director of the National Coalition of Abortion Providers, had stated in November 1995 that "women had these abortions only in the most extreme circumstances of life endangerment or fetal anomaly." However, he later admitted that his own contacts with many of the physicians performing intact D&X procedures found that the vast majority were done not in response to extreme medical conditions but on healthy mothers and healthy fetuses.

In newspaper interviews, physicians who use the technique acknowledged performing thousands of such procedures a year. One facility reported that physicians used intact D&X on at least half of the estimated 3,000 abortions

Excerpted from M. LeRoy Sprang and Mark G. Neerhof, "Rationale for Banning Abortions Late in Pregnancy," *Journal of the American Medical Association*, August 26, 1998. Reprinted with permission from the American Medical Association.

they perform each year on fetuses between 20 and 24 weeks' gestation. In another report, Dayton, Ohio, physician Martin Haskell, who had performed more than 700 partial-birth abortions, stated that most of his abortions are elective in that 20- to 24-week range and that "probably 20% are for genetic reasons, and the other 80% are purely elective." The late James T. McMahon, MD, of Los Angeles, California, detailed for the US Congress his experience with more than 2000 partial-birth abortion procedures. He classified only 9% of that total as involving maternal health indications (of which the most common was depression), and 56% were for "fetal flaws" that included many nonlethal disorders, some as minor as a cleft lip.

> *"There exist no credible studies on [late-term abortion] that evaluate or attest to its safety."*

These accounts indicate that the estimates of performing intact D&X have been grossly understated. The absence of accurate data is at least partly due to the erratic nature of the data collection process. The Centers for Disease Control and Prevention (CDC), in Atlanta, Georgia, collects annual abortion data, but these data are incomplete for several reasons. First, all states do not provide abortion-related information to the CDC. Second, data gathered vary widely from state to state, with some states lacking information on as many as 40% to 50% of abortions performed within their jurisdictions. Third, the categories CDC uses to report the method of abortion do not differentiate between dilation and evacuation (D&E) and intact D&X.

Conflicting information about intact D&X and its frequency catalyzed prominent medical organizations to evaluate the procedure. In 1996, the American College of Obstetricians and Gynecologists (ACOG) convened a special committee to review it. According to the ACOG panel, intact D&X has been defined to consist of 4 elements: (1) the deliberate dilation of the cervix, usually over a sequence of days; (2) instrumental conversion of the fetus to a footling breech; (3) breech extraction of the body, excepting the head; and (4) partial evacuation of the intercranial contents of a living fetus to effect vaginal delivery of a dead but otherwise intact fetus.

An ACOG policy statement emanating from the review declared that the select panel "could identify no circumstances under which this procedure . . . , would be the only option to save the life or preserve the health of the woman" and that "an intact D&X, however, may be the best or most appropriate procedure in a particular circumstance to save the life or preserve the health of a woman, and only the doctor, in consultation with the patient, based upon the woman's particular circumstances can make this decision." However, no specific examples of circumstances under which intact D&X would be the most appropriate procedure were given.

There exist no credible studies on intact D&X that evaluate or attest to its safety. The procedure is not recognized in medical textbooks nor is it taught in medical schools or in obstetrics and gynecology residencies. Intact D&X poses serious medical risks to the mother. Patients who undergo an intact D&X are at risk for the potential complications associated with any surgical midtrimester termination, including hemorrhage, infection, and uterine perforation. However, intact D&X places these patients at increased risk of 2 additional complications. First, the risk of uterine rupture may be increased. An integral part of the D&X procedure is an internal podalic version, during which the physician instrumentally reaches into the uterus, grasps the fetus' feet, and pulls the feet down into the cervix, thus converting the lie to a footling breech. The internal version carries risk of uterine rupture, abruption, amniotic fluid embolus [obstruction], and trauma to the uterus. According to Williams Obstetrics, "there are very few, if any, indications for internal podalic version other than for delivery of a second twin."

The second potential complication of intact D&X is the risk of iatrogenic [physician-induced] laceration and secondary hemorrhage. Following internal version and partial breech extraction, scissors are forced into the base of the fetal skull while it is lodged in the birth canal. This blind procedure risks maternal injury from laceration of the uterus or cervix by the scissors and could result in severe bleeding and the threat of shock or even maternal death. These risks have not been adequately quantified.

None of these risks are medically necessary because other procedures are available to physicians who deem it necessary to perform an abortion late in pregnancy. As ACOG policy

> *"None of these risks are medically necessary because other procedures are available."*

states clearly, intact D&X is never the only procedure available. Some clinicians have considered intact D&X necessary when hydrocephalus is present. However, a hydrocephalic fetus could be aborted by first draining the excess fluid from the fetal skull through ultrasound-guided cephalocentesis. Some physicians who perform abortions have been concerned that a ban on late abortions would affect their ability to provide other abortion services. Because of the proposed changes in federal legislation, it is clear that only intact D&X would be banned.

Fetal Considerations

The centers necessary for pain perception develop early in the second trimester. Although fetal pain cannot be measured, acute stress in the fetus is indexed by blood flow redistribution to the brain, as shown by Doppler studies of human fetuses of at least 18 weeks' gestation undergoing invasive procedures that involve penetration of the fetal trunk. Fetal hormonal stress response to needling of the intra-abdominal portion of the umbilical vein can be measured from as early as 23 weeks' gestation.

The majority of intact D&X procedures are performed on periviable [nearly viable] fetuses. When infants of similar gestational ages are delivered, pain management is an important part of the care rendered to them in the intensive care nursery. However, with intact D&X, pain management is not provided for the fetus, who is literally within inches of being delivered. Forcibly incising the cranium with a scissors and then suctioning out the intracranial contents is certainly excrutiatingly painful. It is beyond ironic that the pain management practiced for an intact D&X on a human fetus would

> *"Forcibly incising the cranium with a scissors and then suctioning out the [brain] is certainly excruciatingly painful."*

not meet federal standards for the humane care of animals used in medical research. The needlessly inhumane treatment of periviable fetuses argues against intact D&X as a means of pregnancy termination.

Ethical Considerations

Intact D&X is most commonly performed between 20 and 24 weeks and thereby raises questions of the potential viability of the fetus. Information from 1988 through 1991 indicates a 15% viability rate at 23 weeks' gestation, 56% at 24 weeks, and 79% at 25 weeks. Recent data . . . indicate an 83% survival rate at 24 weeks and an 89% survival rate at 25 weeks.

Beyond the argument of potential viability, many prochoice organizations and individuals assert that a woman should maintain control over that which is part of her own body (i.e., the autonomy argument). In this context, the physical position of the fetus with respect to the mother's body becomes relevant. However, once the fetus is outside the woman's body, the autonomy argument is invalid. The intact D&X procedure involves literally delivering the fetus so that only the head remains within the cervix. At this juncture, the fetus is merely inches from being delivered and obtaining full legal rights of personhood under the US Constitution. What happens when, as must occasionally occur during the performance of an intact D&X, the fetal head inadvertently slips out of the mother and a live infant is fully delivered? For this reason, many otherwise prochoice individuals have found intact D&X too close to infanticide to ethically justify its continued use.

Professional, Legislative, and Public Concerns

An extraordinary medical consensus has emerged that intact D&X is neither necessary nor the safest method for late-term abortion. In addition to American Medical Association (AMA) and ACOG policy statements, Warren Hern, MD, author of *Abortion Practice* has questioned the efficacy of intact D&X. "I have very serious reservations about this procedure. . . . You really can't defend it. . . . I would dispute any statement that this is the safest procedure to use." Hern states that turning the fetus to a breech position is "potentially dangerous." In

Illinois, a November 1996 survey of all physicians in Sangamon County (the city of Springfield and surrounding area) demonstrated that 91% of more than 180 respondents supported a ban of intact D&X. In April 1997, more than 200 physician delegates who attended the Illinois State Medical Society annual meeting voted to support a ban on intact D&X. The AMA established its own committee to study partial-birth abortion and adopted the recommendations of that committee's report, as well as an official position of support for . . . federal legislation banning partial-birth abortions that the AMA worked to improve and clarify prior to passage.

Legislative bodies across the United States have decided that intact D&X is not appropriate. In fact, 28 states have approved a ban, and Congress also overwhelmingly voted to ban the procedure with strong bipartisan support. [Clinton has vetoed the legislation and Congress has been unable to override his veto.] When Illinois' prochoice Gov. Jim Edgar signed legislation enacting a ban in July 1997, he described the measure as one that "essentially prohibits a barbaric procedure that is repugnant to me and to almost all Illinoisans. I believe such a restriction is a proper, reasonable and humane public policy." Public opinion surveys demonstrate wide support for banning partial-birth abortion when the procedure is described to those interviewed. According to the *Chicago Tribune*, "The American people have learned enough about partial-birth abortions to know that they should be stopped." New York Democratic Sen. Daniel Patrick Moynihan, whose legislative record is neither prolife nor conservative, has declared, "It [intact D&X] is as close to infanticide as anything I have come upon." Former Surgeon General C. Everett Koop captured the dilemma: ". . . in no way can I twist my mind to see that the late-term abortion as described—you know, partial birth and then destruction of the unborn child before the head is born—is a medical necessity for the mother. It certainly can't be a necessity for the baby.". . .

> *"Many otherwise prochoice individuals have found intact D&X too close to infanticide to ethically justify its continued use."*

Professional Obligations

Medical professionals have an obligation to thoughtfully consider the medical and ethical issues surrounding pregnancy termination, particularly with respect to intact D&X and late-term abortions. Having done so, we conclude the following: (1) Intact D&X (partial-birth abortion) should not be performed because it is needlessly risky, inhumane, and ethically unacceptable. This procedure is closer to infanticide than it is to abortion. (2) Abortions in the periviable period (currently 23 weeks) and beyond should be considered unethical, unless the fetus has a condition incompatible with prolonged survival or if the mother's life is endangered by the pregnancy. (3) If a maternal medical condition in the periviable period indicates pregnancy termination, the physician should wait, if the medical condition permits, until fetal survival is probable and then proceed with delivery. Such medical decisions must be individualized.

Physicians must preserve their role as healing, compassionate, caring professionals, while recognizing their ethical obligation to care for both the woman and the unborn child.

Chapter 4

Should Protesters Target Abortion Clinics and Providers?

Abortion Clinic Protests: An Overview

by Charles S. Clark

About the author: *Charles S. Clark is a staff writer for the* CQ Researcher.

In the predawn darkness of June 4, 1994, three men and two women methodically set about creating havoc at a Milwaukee abortion clinic. Using an elaborate construction of chains, concrete blocks and iron pipes, they secured themselves to two cars blocking the clinic entrance. Inside one of the cars, three protesters had removed the floorboards and were sitting on the pavement so the car could not be dragged away. Their arms were encased in pipes set in concrete blocks. The other two protesters were chained to the outside of the other car and to a concrete-filled drum.

Two dozen firefighters worked for four hours to extricate the protesters, using metal cutters and jackhammers. But the protest had the desired effect: The appointments of 17 patients had to be canceled.

Though such blockades have become frequent in recent years, this one marked a turning point: It was the first test of the tough, new federal law known as FACE (for Freedom of Access to Clinic Entrances Act). In January, the five protesters were sentenced under FACE to up to six months in prison and fines of up to $2,500.

If the abortion rights community was cheered by the beefed-up enforcement, the new sense of security didn't last. On December 30, 1994, two abortion clinics in Brookline, Massachusetts, were raked with gunfire from a .22 caliber semiautomatic rifle, killing two receptionists and wounding five other employees. John Salvi III, a 22-year-old hairdresser, was charged with the assaults.

Since 1977, there have been at least 1,712 acts of violence against abortion clinics, including 40 bombings and 92 cases of arson, according to the National Abortion Federation (NAF). In 1994, there were a record four murders and eight attempted murders, the group says. More than half of the estimated 1,500 U.S. clinics experienced either death threats, stalkings, bombings, invasions, ar-

Excerpted from Charles S. Clark, "Abortion Clinic Protests: The Issues," *CQ Researcher*, April 7, 1995. Reprinted with permission from *CQ Researcher*.

son or blockades in the first seven months of 1994, according to the Feminist Majority Foundation. Five California clinics were hit by arson [in early 1995].

The chain of violence prompted Attorney General Janet Reno to assemble a task force [in 1994] to determine whether there is a criminal conspiracy among antiabortion activists.

Common Tactics

Though only a fraction of anti-abortion activists defend the extremist doctrine of "justifiable homicide," many protesters have intensified their disruption tactics in recent years. Besides the clinic blockades (or "rescues"), protests now include flooding clinics with foul-smelling butyric acid, putting glue in the locks of clinic doors, picketing abortion doctors' homes and harassing their children on the way to school.

Also common are efforts to generate malpractice lawsuits against clinics. A Dallas, Texas, group called Life Dynamics Inc. has mounted 71 cases so far, aided by its nationwide network of 600 lawyers and 500 expert witnesses.

Most common of all at many abortion clinics are the lines of protesters chanting on sidewalks and offering impromptu "counseling" to the arriving women. "No issue since the Vietnam War or the civil rights movement so galvanized vast numbers of 'ordinary' people to street-level protest," says a report from a national law enforcement research group.

The Impact

The impact of the protests—both peaceful and violent—has been thunderous. The Planned Parenthood Federation of America, which operates nearly 1,000 health centers, says that for the first time in its 79 years it is providing pregnancy services under armed guard—and considering installing metal detectors and bulletproof glass. The U.S. Marshals Service warns clinic staffers to be wary of strange packages and to remove their names from home mailboxes. More and more clinics are using trained escorts to help women pick their way around protesters.

Most significant, "There's an impression that a lot of doctors are retiring prematurely from the abortion business because of violence, the notoriety and perceived threats to their families," says Randall Whitney, an obstetrician-gynecologist in Daytona Beach, Florida. His home and clinic have been picketed, and he now wears a bulletproof vest and carries a weapon in his van.

> *"Since 1977, there have been at least 1,712 acts of violence against abortion clinics."*

"We offer first- and second-trimester abortions, but we are diversifying our services," which may make his clinic less of a target, he says.

Kate Michelman, president of the National Abortion and Reproductive Rights Action League (NARAL), argues that when the anti-abortion movement "lost access to the White House and hence the Supreme Court, they decided to achieve their goals through targeting doctors and clinics." As a result, she says, the availability of abortion "is in serious jeopardy."

Statistically, the 1.5 million pregnancies terminated in the United States in 1992 marked the lowest incidence of abortion in 13 years, according to a January 1995 report by the Alan Guttmacher Institute in New York City. Analysts differ, however, over whether the dropoff is attributable more to the closing of clinics, changes in attitudes or a decline in the number of women of reproductive age. What is clear is that the number of counties with an abortion provider has fallen 31 percent, from 714 in 1978 to 495 in 1992, and the number of hospitals providing abortions dropped from 1,040 in 1988 to 855 in 1992.

Placing Blame

The declining availability of abortion services—combined with the murders of abortion clinic workers and the damage to clinics—has compelled many abortion rights activists to blame the anti-abortion movement as a whole. "Words kill," declared a full-page ad in *The New York Times* taken out by Planned Parenthood of New York City after the Brookline murders. It called for a permanent moratorium on clinic protests.

"I don't think incendiary rhetoric [about 'baby killing'] is non-violent," says the Rev. Katherine Hancock Ragsdale, president of the Religious

"The impact of the protests—both peaceful and violent—has been thunderous."

Coalition for Reproductive Choice. "Violent rhetoric leads to violent action, and the first step is disrespect for the consciences of people they disagree with. This rhetoric trivializes, dehumanizes and demonizes us. It marks us as fair game for violence."

Opinion polls indicate that the general public agrees. In recent years, only about 15 percent of Americans have thought that abortion under all circumstances should be made illegal. And just after the Brookline shootings, a Yankelovich Partners poll for *Time*-CNN showed that 61 percent agreed that the actions of antiabortion groups encourage violence, while 57 percent said the murders made them feel less sympathetic to groups who oppose abortion.

But Helen Alvare, a spokeswoman for the National Conference of Catholic Bishops, says the level of violence gets exaggerated and that many clinics label as harassment what in the majority of cases is legitimate protest. "I've traveled to clinics in 47 states, and most protests involve a few people saying prayers on the sidewalk or holding signs," she says. "But the clippings I get from 100 newspapers describe only those that are large and confrontational. And pro-lifers also get attacked—in Ohio last year, one had his car firebombed—but the newspapers don't cover that."

Other anti-abortion activists think that the enactment of FACE—coupled with the Republican takeover of Congress—has galvanized their movement. And they point to sidewalk clinic protesters' success in non-violently persuading women to abandon planned abortions.

"Every time we go to a clinic, we have at least one turnaway, and oftentimes five or six if there are no escorts," says Tim Murphy, research director for the Pro-Life Action League. "Everyone says we go out and shout, 'Don't kill your baby,' but if we did, no one would listen. There are people who do that, but we tell them not to, and they're usually the type of person that doesn't stick with us."

The Key Questions

As activists on both sides of the abortion debate continue their struggles, these are some of the key questions being asked:

Is there a conspiracy linking the attacks on abortion clinics? At the federal courthouse in Alexandria, Virginia, a grand jury empaneled by Attorney General Reno in fall 1994 has been meeting periodically to explore whether a conspiracy has targeted the abortion industry with violence.

Several anti-abortion activists questioned by the secret panel because of their ties to the movement's "justifiable homicide" faction called the investigation "modern-day McCarthyism." Terry Sullivan, an activist from Colorado, said the civil rights and anti–Vietnam War movements "had people who advocated violent overthrows and acted on that. [The pro-life movement has] a spectrum of philosophical positions about the role of non-violence and violence in protests, but it's a philosophical debate."

One reason for the belief in a conspiracy is that the protesters arrested for violence seem well-funded. "They all travel, come to memorial services, make cash contributions to each other and, though many of them who have children remain personally poor [as a legal strategy], they keep paying fines and taking liens on their property as they go in and out of jail," says Allie Harper, executive administrator of the Hillcrest chain of abortion clinics in the Northeast.

"We don't have information to prove a conspiracy, but patterns and behaviors give us reasons to believe in an organized plan," says NAF spokeswoman Gina Shaw. "It may be a loosely organized plan, which is to their benefit."

> *"Only about 15 percent of Americans have thought that abortion under all circumstances should be made illegal."*

"The legal notion of a conspiracy, in which more than one person moves toward an illegal act, has to show an intention," notes Kathryn Kolbert, vice president of the Center for Reproductive Law and Policy in New York. "And the conspirators don't necessarily have to have actually attempted the act. But there's a big difference between what's likely in the real world and what can be proven in court."

Indeed, more than 25 years ago, in a case involving the Ku Klux Klan, the Supreme Court struggled to balance the rights of free speech against potential danger to public safety. It ruled in *Brandenburg v. Ohio* that mere advocacy of violence is protected by the First Amendment, unless the threat of lawless action is imminent.

> *"Many clinics label as harassment what in the majority of cases is legitimate protest."*

Still, Kolbert says, "it is incumbent on law enforcers to ask whether there are interconnections between 55–60 events involving use of butyric acid at clinics across the country, or three and four arsons in California in the same week with the same modus operandi.

"The importance of the FACE law is that it says this is no longer just individuals or groups exercising their right to protest but a federal crime. No one, for example, would say that after the [1993 World Trade Center bombing] that if police picked up only the guy who drove the car, there's no need for more effort. The government has an obligation" to fully investigate. . . .

Conflicting Theories

Abortion rights advocates say their longtime suspicion that the anti-abortion movement has a guidebook on violence was confirmed when authorities searching [abortion protester Rachelle "Shelley"] Shannon's house found an anonymously published text calling itself a "how-to manual of means to disrupt and ultimately destroy Satan's power to kill our children." Entitled "The Army of God," it offers technical advice on such tactics as cutting off the thumbs of abortion doctors; parking old, locked cars on clinic property; clogging the sewage lines of abortion clinics; and using plastic explosives, fingerprint-proof guns and arson to destroy abortion clinic "death camps."

While such advice may not be proof of a conspiracy, it may explain some similarities in the protesters' tactics.

Anti-abortion activists insist that killers such as Paul Hill and Michael Griffin, convicted of murdering Pensacola abortion doctor David Gunn, were "nuts" who acted alone. "I've been exposed to hundreds of thousands of pro-lifers," says Judie Brown, president of the American Life League. "There may be one or two fanatics, and no one can control the activities or behavior of everyone, but 99.9 percent of us are law-abiding, noble people."

Others in the movement suggest that some violence is generated by authorities or abortion rights advocates. In a recent essay in the antiabortion monthly *Life Advocate*, activist Paul deParrie speculates that the FBI had planted a threatening note sent to an abortion rights activist signed "The Lord's Avenger."

"It could mean that some element of the FBI was trying to discredit pro-lifers in general," he wrote. "Or it could mean that the Justice Department considered pro-lifers to be 'in the same league' as other dissident groups and was not above using violence to play Left against Right."

Murphy of the Pro-Life Action League cites the 1986 case of Frank Mendiola, a nephew of Cesar Chavez, the late farmworkers' activist, who pleaded guilty to phoning in fake bomb threats to clinics. "This story confirms what many of us have been saying all along," league founder Joseph Scheidler wrote in a memo to fellow activists; "the abortionists are probably the ones calling in many of the registered bomb threats."

As the conspiracy investigation continues, the Justice Department is overseeing daily police surveillance of core anti-abortion activists. Spokesman Tom Hill of the Bureau of Alcohol, Tobacco and Firearms (ATF) says that dozens of criminal cases remain unsolved, including arsons and bombings that have caused individual clinics upwards of $1 million in damage. Hill says that "all the people arrested since the 1980s" have been investigated, and "none have been connected in any way . . . with a national conspiracy."

The same people, however, have been linked to earlier violence or "to regional conspiracies," Hill says. "Some people come together for deep-seated religious reasons and then cross over the line. It's hard to prove. It would be easier if there were a national conspiracy, which is not to say these people are not violating the law; we're looking at it.". . .

Who Is to Blame?

Should the whole anti-abortion movement share blame for clinic violence? In January 1995, days after Salvi was arrested in Norfolk, Virginia, the Reverend Donald Spitz, an anti-abortion activist, stood outside Salvi's jail and shouted. "We love you! Thank you for what you did in the name of Jesus!"

Another anti-abortion protester, Donna Bray of Bowie, Maryland, the wife of convicted clinic bomber Michael Bray, was quoted in January 1995 on National Public Radio as saying that nonviolent anti-abortion advocates should reconsider their approach because "non-violence has not worked."

Although it resoundingly condemned the violence, the National Conference of Catholic Bishops split over the Salvi episode. Cardinal Bernard Law of Boston called for a moratorium on all clinic protests, but Cardinal John O'Connor of New York disagreed, saying a moratorium would be appropriate only when accompanied by a moratorium on abortions.

The National Right to Life Committee issued a statement saying that it "strongly opposes any use of violence as a means of stopping the violence that has killed more than 31 million unborn children since 1973." But, it added, linking the violence to those speaking "in favor of the right to live . . . is like blaming the civil rights movement—and all those who courageously spoke in favor of the rights of African-

> *"One reason for the belief in a conspiracy is that the protesters arrested for violence seem well-funded."*

Americans—for the riots or deaths that were a part of that era."

Around the country, however, divisions within the movement developed. "For the first time, there's going to be a rift in the pro-life movement," said Teri Reisser, executive director of the Right to Life League of Southern California, promising to alert authorities about other anti-abortion activists who advocate violence. "We will not embrace those who talk of justifiable homicide in our ranks."

"Wanted" Posters

The Right to Life organization in Cincinnati took a more aggressive approach that drew criticism from abortion rights activists. It published 65,000 copies of a newsletter containing photographs and home addresses of area abortion doctors. 'This is a very powerful, persuasive way for some to realize maybe they've forgotten what it means to be a physician," wrote Barbara Willke, the group's cofounder. Cincinnati's Planned Parenthood group called the act "dangerous and irresponsible."

Eleanor Smeal [of the Feminist Majority Foundation] noted that until the newsletter's distribution, major anti-abortion groups had eschewed such tactics, which critics liken to putting doctors' pictures on "wanted" posters. "Given the current extremes," she says, "this [action] is troublesome." When asked about the newsletter, a spokesman for the National Right to Life Committee reiterated that it opposes violence.

> *"Words are abused by many people, but when someone sets his mind on a violent act, it is not done because of language."*

The Religious Coalition for Reproductive Choice argued after the Brookline shootings that the heated rhetoric used by anti-abortion groups makes them partially responsible for ensuing violence. "When leaders compare abortion to the Holocaust, abortion providers to Nazis and anti-clinic terrorists to resistance fighters, they cross the line that separates passionate debate from inciting violence," coalition leaders said in a January 17, 1995, open letter to anti-abortion religious leaders.

Michelman goes even further in placing blame. "Because of their incendiary rhetoric," she says, "the major anti-abortion groups are responsible. You move along a continuum from the American Life League, the National Right to Life Committee and the Family Research Council saying, 'Abortion is murder,' and then you get to Operation Rescue and the Army of God."

Anti-abortion groups reject being linked to violent extremists. "We have condemned the violence as repugnant," says the Reverend Patrick Mahoney, director of the Washington-based Christian Defense Coalition. "We wouldn't let Hill or Salvi attend our rallies."

In an encyclical letter released March 30, 1995, Pope John Paul II strongly opposed legislation permitting abortion but condemned violence in the anti-abortion movement. "When, in accordance with their principles, such movements act resolutely, but without resorting to violence, they promote a wider and more profound consciousness of the value of life, and evoke and bring about a more determined commitment to its defense," he said. . . .

Brown of the American Life League contends that "there have also been violent attacks on pro-lifers. My life has been threatened." As for the activists' rhetoric, "'Baby killer' is an accurate term for those who perform abortions," she says. The concept of justifiable homicide against doctors, however, "is abominable," she says. "Words are abused by many people, but when someone sets his mind on a violent act, it is not done because of language. Paul Hill had a mental problem that made him lose respect for life." . . .

> *"To many abortion rights advocates, even peaceful protests create ill will."*

Brown acknowledges that the violence has been a setback to the antiabortion movement. "But this is all within the context of a real battle, like civil rights and slavery," she says. "There will be people on both sides who lose [their sanity]. The answer is to pray for both."

Peaceful Clinic Protests

Are peaceful clinic protests a legitimate tactic in the abortion struggle? When anti-abortion protesters launch a "rescue" to shut down a clinic, the noise level can be high, notes Michael Schwartz, director of the Life Advocacy Alliance, which lobbies for independent, anti-abortion groups. But most activities at clinics are not noisy, he says. "They involve picketing, praying or engaging prospective patients in conversation to show them alternatives." What's more, "Peaceful prayer vigils on the sidewalk virtually guarantee that the clinic won't be shot at," he says. "Deliberate assassins like Griffin and Hill would never try it if there are pro-lifers around."

But to many abortion rights advocates, even peaceful protests create ill will. "I haven't seen many peaceful protests," says Reverend Ragsdale of the Religious Coalition for Reproductive Choice. "Fists may not be flying at every one, but the level of hostility, incivility and disrespect is clearly violent in and of itself. I see a carpet of lies and misleading statements undergirding a movement that enables them to dismiss us and our faith commitment."

For example, Ragsdale says, while the Bible doesn't speak to abortion, she and others in her interfaith coalition interpret passages as permitting abortion. "It's an honest disagreement," she says, "but the other side believes their interpretation is fact." She also objects to anti-abortion protesters "calling embryos and fetuses 'babies,' as if that were scientific with no moral distinction between them. If the protesters were all just elderly women praying, no one would be upset," Ragsdale says. "But these people are barring doors, screaming epithets and carrying gigantic pictures of bloody fetuses."

Chapter 4

Beyond Clinic Protests

Clinic staff object to the way protesters carry their cause beyond the site of the clinics themselves. "Doctors are harassed at home," says Shaw. "Their whole family gets targeted in restaurants, or in the grocery store. They get pictures of their children sent to them in the mail, with notes saying, 'We're watching you.'"

In his primer, *Closed: 99 Ways to Stop Abortion,* Scheidler instructs activists on how to set up anti-abortion counseling centers next door to abortion clinics; how to "blitz" clinic lobbies and replace their pamphlets on abortion with anti-abortion literature; and how to use license plate numbers to trace the home addresses of clinic employees. "We go to the homes of abortionists and to places they work other than the clinics precisely because they do not like it," he writes. "They usually are not proud of being abortionists, and often they even guard from their community the fact that they are involved in abortion."

The Pro-Life Action League's Murphy, says the most effective tactic for clinic protesters is known as the "Chicago method"—researching a clinic's malpractice record and presenting arriving patients with written summaries. "We write up episodes of uterine perforation, cervical lacerations, incomplete abortions or sometimes hysterectomies that have been performed on young girls," Murphy says. "And we photocopy articles on unsanitary conditions. If you talk about the baby, the woman can't run away fast enough, but if you say, 'This isn't a safe place' and offer a card, it works."

So-called sidewalk counselors who are trained by the Pro-Life Action League learn that the most common questions on the mind of a woman or girl arriving for an abortion are "Will it hurt?" and "Does it look like a baby?" Jeannie Hill, a Wheat Ridge, Colorado, nurse, suggests in a handbook on sidewalk counseling that anti-abortion protesters address the women with such comments as, "Your baby's heart is beating now, it won't be in an hour," or "Hold your baby very close, he needs you now."

> *"[Abortion protesters] go to the homes of abortionists and to places they work other than the clinics precisely because they do not like it."*

Once a woman seeking an abortion has been stopped from going to a clinic, "it is absolutely vital to the success of the technique that you not disclose that you are an anti-abortionist or that the agency you are taking your clients to will not give them an abortion or a referral to one," advises another league publication. "If they ask, say, 'They'll give you all the help you need.'"

Shaw says the success rates of protests and sidewalk counseling have been greatly exaggerated. "Every time a car slows down and a woman doesn't come in, they say it's a turnaround, but I haven't seen them change anyone's mind," she says. "Some women who're ambivalent, at the behest of a clinic counselor, go home and think it over. But they're not turned around by some crazy stranger on the sidewalk."

Smeal, whose Feminist Majority Foundation has trained some 37,000 volunteer clinic defenders, says: "I've been on the lines, and I've never seen a turnaway. There are lots of people there on our side too, and we don't let the protesters get that close to these women. Most women are running in, and they're often with a friend." She adds, "Sidewalk counselor is a deceitful term. Real counseling is done in a voluntary atmosphere, in which there is some relationship. These people run at the women and try to grab, lecture, preach and yell."

But Michele Arocha Allen, communications director for the National Right to Life Committee, says the counselors generally are "compassionate and caring" women who may have had abortions themselves. And, she adds, they provide information on fetal development that women [considering abortions] can't get from clinics.

Many anti-abortion activists say they don't approve of all tactics that are used in the name of the cause. "I have no problem with reminding an abortionist that what he does is reprehensible, but I'd feel uneasy going after doctors' children, who are non-combatants," says Schwartz. "At first, I thought the rescues were a good idea because they showed the media how serious and non-violent we are. But now it has become a costly World War I of trench warfare, with people deliberately breaking the trespassing laws. I mean, what's the point of 300 arrests?"

"We haven't done a detailed list on what's allowed," says Alvare of the bishops conference. "We do say that pro-lifers should act at all times as if they are wearing a pro-life bumper sticker, so that everyone can tell they're pro-life by their exemplary behavior. If you want a pro-life world, you have to make it, or else you're no better than an abortion rights activist."

Killing Abortion Providers Is Justifiable Homicide

by Paul J. Hill

About the author: *Paul J. Hill, a former minister and the executive director of the pro-life organization Defensive Action, was convicted of murdering Dr. John Britton and his escort.*

I didn't normally stand in the middle of the driveway leading to the abortion clinic. But this day was different. I was determined to do everything in my power to prevent John Britton from killing any children that day—or ever again. I had made up my mind that the clinic door would not close and lock behind the abortionist—protecting him as he dismembered over thirty unborn children.

Taking this action first occurred to me eight days earlier. I had a business touching up cars at dealerships and used car lots. I was working at a car lot in the afternoon, wondering who would act next, when the idea of acting myself struck; it hit hard. During the next two or three hours, as I continued to work in a distracted manner, I began to consider what would happen if I were to shoot an abortionist.

The man who had previously shot an abortionist in Pensacola in March 1993, Michael Griffin, had been dismissed because what he said about shooting abortionists contradicted his actions. But few people considered me to be vacillating or self-contradictory.

After serving as a Presbyterian minister for seven years, I had left my former denomination because they inconsistently provided baptism to infants while denying them communion. I had moved my family to Pensacola to join a Presbyterian church that practiced both infant baptism and infant communion.

I was also known for having taken a uniform stand on defending both born and unborn children with force. Two days after Griffin killed Dr. Gunn, I called the *Phil Donahue* show and told them I supported the shooting. Three days later, I appeared on *Donahue* with the abortionist's son, and compared killing

Excerpted from Paul J. Hill, "Why I Shot an Abortionist," *Prayer and Action News*, December 22, 1997. Reprinted with permission from the author.

Dr. Gunn to killing a Nazi concentration camp "doctor."

I then wrote a paper justifying the shooting, had an article published, and led numerous national pro-life leaders in signing a statement justifying Griffin's actions. I subsequently appeared on ABC's *Nightline,* and justified Shelly Shannon's shooting of an abortionist in August 1993, in Wichita, Kansas.

Fighting for Life

During the *Nightline* broadcast, I defended the shooting on the basis of the Sixth Commandment (which not only forbids murder, but also requires the means necessary to prevent murder). It's not enough to refrain from committing murder; innocent people must also be protected.

Most people don't realize that legal abortion requires a sin of omission by forbidding people to intervene as mass murder is taking place. By legalizing abortion the government has robbed you of your right to defend your own relatives and neighbors from a bloody death. It's as though a machine gunner is taking aim on bound peasants, huddled before a mass grave, and you are forbidden to stop him. In much the same way, the abortionist's knife is pressed to the throat of the unborn, and you are forbidden to stop him. It's as though the police are holding a gun on you, and forcing you to submit to murder— possibly the murder of your own child or grandchild.

> *"It's not enough to refrain from committing murder; innocent people must also be protected."*

And not only does God require us to defend helpless children, this duty is also inalienable. When the government will not perform this duty on the people's behalf it necessarily reverts to the people. To deny this is to put men in the place of God, and leave helpless children undefended. If the people's children will not be defended by the government, they must be defended by the people, or they will not be defended at all.

And if you want your fellow citizens, and the government, to recognize this duty, you must assert it. The outrage is not that some people use the means necessary to defend the unborn, but that since most people deny that this duty exists, the government will not perform it on the people's behalf.

Striking Results

When I first appeared on *Donahue*, I took the position that Griffin's killing of Dr. Gunn was justified, but I asked the audience to suspend judgment as to whether it had been wise. I realized later, however, that using the force necessary to defend the unborn gives credibility, urgency, and direction to the pro-life movement which it has lacked, and which it needs in order to prevail.

I realized that using force to stop abortion is the same means that God has used to stop similar atrocities throughout history. In the book of Esther for instance, Ahasuerus, the king of Persia, passed a law in 473 B.C. allowing the Persians to kill their Jewish neighbors. But the Jews didn't passively submit; their use of defensive force prevented a calamity of immense proportions. In much the same way, when abortion was first legalized in our nation, if the people had resisted this atrocity with the means necessary it would have saved millions of people from a bloody death. It's not unwise or unspiritual, thus, to use the means that God has appointed for keeping His commandments; rather, it's presumptuous to neglect these means, and expect Him to work apart from them.

> *"I realized that using force to stop abortion is the same means that God has used to stop similar atrocities throughout history."*

I realized that a large number of extremely important things would be accomplished by my shooting another abortionist in Pensacola. This would put the pro-life rhetoric about defending born and unborn children equally into practice. It would bear witness to the full humanity of the unborn as nothing else could. It would also open people's eyes to the enormous consequences of abortion—not only for the unborn, but also for the government which had sanctioned it, and those required to resist it. This would convict millions of people of their past neglect, and also spur many to future obedience. I also realized that this would help to force the silent masses to either pull for those who defend abortionists, or those who defend the unborn.

But, most importantly, I knew that this would uphold the truth of the gospel at the precise point of Satan's current attack (the abortionist's knife). While most Christians firmly profess the duty to defend born children with force (which is not being disputed by the government) most of these professors have neglected the duty to similarly defend the unborn. They are steady everywhere on the battlefield except where the battle currently rages. I was certain that if I took my stand at this point, others would join with me, and the Lord would eventually bring about a great victory.

With thoughts like these racing through my mind, I finished my work that Thursday afternoon and drove home. I continued to secretly consider shooting an abortionist, half hoping it would not appear as plausible after I had given it more thought.

A Window of Opportunity

The next morning, Friday, as was my practice, I went to the abortion clinic (the Ladies Center). I arrived at about eight o'clock, the time that many of the mothers began arriving. I was usually the first protester there, but that day another activist had arrived first. What was even more unusual was, after discrete questioning, I learned that he had been there when the abortionist had arrived, about 7:30. More importantly, I discovered that the abortionist had arrived a few minutes *prior* to the police security guard. This information was like a bright green light, signaling me on.

For months my wife had planned to take our children on a trip to visit my parents, and to take my son to summer camp. She planned to leave that coming Wednesday morning and return the following week. I would have the remainder of the day that she left, and all of Thursday, to prepare to act on Friday, eight days after the idea first struck me. All I had to do was hide my intentions from my wife for a few days until she left. If I did not act during her planned trip (since I could not have kept my feelings from her for long) she would almost certainly develop suspicions later, and my plans would be spoiled for fear of implicating her. I could not hope for a better opportunity than the one immediately before me. God had opened a window of opportunity, and it appeared that I had been appointed to step through it.

Remembering God's Promise

Saturday afternoon, the second day after I began to consider taking action, we went as a family to the beach. My wife, Karen, and I enjoyed the beach in the afternoon.

Our three children were delighted with the outing. My son was nine, and my two daughters were six and three. We dug in the sand, splashed in the water, and walked along the beach on the wet sand. All the while I weighed my plans in my mind, being careful not to arouse suspicion.

This was a heartrending experience that almost overwhelmed me. I doubted I would ever take my family to the beach like this again. I would be in prison—separated from my beautiful wife and children. The sight of them walking along the beach, so happy and serene, and the contrasting thought of being removed from them was startling, almost breathtaking. Surging waves of emotion swept over me—threatening to start tears in my eyes.

I could not allow my emotions to show. To retain control, I lifted my heart to the Lord in praise and faith. As long as I responded to the swelling pain in my chest with praise, I could rise above it, and still see things clearly—and what a strikingly beautiful sight it was. Somehow, responding to the pain with intense praise turned it into joy—a joy as clean and clear as the sand and sky. As I lifted my heart and eyes upward, I was reminded of God's promise to bless Abraham, and grant him descendants as numerous as the stars in the sky. I claimed that promise as my own, and rejoiced with all my might, lest my eyes become clouded with tears and they betray me.

> *"God had opened a window of opportunity, and it appeared that I had been appointed to step through it."*

All my paternal instincts were stirred as I played with my children. They enjoyed their father's attention. I took them one by one, each in turn, into water over their heads as they clung to my neck. As I carried and supported each child in the water, it was as though I was offering them to God as Abraham offered his son.

I also admired the beauty and grace of my wife. I knew that, by God's grace, she would be able to cope with my being incarcerated, but it was soul wrenching to think of being separated from her—though I knew our relationship would continue.

Though I would almost surely be removed from my precious family, I knew that God would somehow work everything out. I would not lose them but only be separated from them. The separation would be painful, but the reward would be great, too great to fathom, it was simply accepted in faith.

An Agonizing Decision

By the time the sun set, the emotions that I had experienced on the beach had ebbed. We brushed the sand from our things and walked back to the car. Neither Karen nor the children seemed alerted to anything. Like a man savoring his last supper, I enjoyed watching them through eyes unknown to them. But I decided to suspend final judgment as to whether I would act until the upcoming Monday. After making my decision, I would then have four days to prepare myself to act on Friday, the day abortions were performed.

The decision was agonizing. I would be leaving my home, children, and wife, but I felt God had given me all I had so that I could return it to Him. Nor was I unmindful of the impact this gift would have, or of the reward. I was also assured, from God's Word, that He would be a Father to my children and sustain my wife.

> *"I was not standing for my own ideas, but God's truths. . . . Who was I to stand in God's way?"*

I had not moved to Pensacola for this purpose, nor had I gotten myself on *Donahue* or *Nightline,* and carried myself through them in my own strength. I certainly had nothing to do with Michael Griffin shooting Dr. Gunn, or the previous Pensacola abortion clinic bombings on Christmas of 1984. I was not standing for my own ideas, but God's truths—the same truths that have stopped blood baths and similar atrocities throughout history. Who was I to stand in God's way? He now held the door open and promised great blessing for obedience. Was I not to step through it?

When Monday arrived, I knew I had to decide. When I went from debating whether to act, in general, to planning a particular act, I felt some relief. I felt that the Lord had placed in my hands a cup whose contents were difficult to swallow, but that it was a task that had to be borne.

My plan was to carry my shotgun from my parked truck to the front of the abortion clinic in a rolled-up poster board protest sign. I would leave the concealed shotgun lying on the ground until the abortionist drove past me into the clinic parking lot.

In spite of my careful plans, the morning of the shooting was not easy. Although I had gone to bed late, I forced myself to rise about 4 A.M. to spend time in prayer and Bible reading, and to prepare myself for the day.

I was fully determined to act, but my usual zest, and the zeal I expected to feel were missing. The lower half of my body was gripped with a gnawing emptiness. It did not occur to me at the time, but I now wonder how Abraham felt as he walked up Mount Moriah to kill his son. It's likely that his soul was crying out, and his body was trying to revolt—mine were.

> *"The people killed had not been innocent, and . . . their deaths had prevented many innocent children from being killed."*

While driving to the clinic, I decided to drive past it first, to see if everything looked normal (I was concerned that someone may have become suspicious and called the police). Just as I approached the clinic, a police cruiser drove by me in the opposite direction. I forced my fears under control as I continued down the road. After driving about an eighth of a mile, it was time to head back, but the truck did not want to turn around; it had to be forced. I could hear the undercarriage groan as I did a tight turn around in an open parking lot. As hard as it was to turn around, I knew I could not continue down the road. Obedience was the only option.

Waiting for the Abortionist

Several months prior to the day of the shooting, *GQ* magazine had interviewed both the pro-life protesters and the pro-choice people who frequented the Ladies Center, including the abortionist. This piece (published in February 1994) discussed the threat I posed to the abortionist, and the possibility of someone, like me, shooting him as he entered the clinic.

I knew from having read this article that the abortionist and his escort were on guard when entering the clinic. Jim Barret, an escort who took his turn driving the abortionist to the clinic, was described as being well armed. He was quoted as saying that, if threatened, he would shoot first and not miss. As it happened, in God's providence, he was the driver killed that day.

As I stood awaiting the abortionist's arrival, I was struggling in fervent prayer to maintain my resolution of heart. At the end, as the moment of his expected arrival approached, I was praying fervently that the police security would not arrive first. I could still find the heart to shoot the abortionist, but, while I knew it would be justified to kill a policeman in order to stop the murderer he was protecting, I did not want to have to do it. I made an earnest and personal request to the Lord to spare me, and the policeman, if possible.

God heard my prayers, and the abortionist arrived prior to the police guard. When I lifted the shotgun, two men were sitting in the front seats of the parked truck; Jim Barret, the escort, was directly between me and the abortionist.

When I finished shooting, I laid the shotgun at my feet and walked away with my hands held out at my sides, awaiting arrest. (I did not want to appear to be threatening anyone when the police arrived.)

Chapter 4

Arrested but Successful

I was relieved when they cuffed me. I gave a hopeful and non-resisting look to the policeman who ordered me under arrest with his drawn handgun. I did not want to be shot, and was glad to be safely in police custody.

When they later led me to the police car, a handful of people had assembled. I spontaneously raised my voice, "One thing's for sure, no innocent people will be killed in that clinic today." The arresting officer incorrectly reported that I had said, ". . . no innocent *babies* will be killed. . . ." I'm certain that he's wrong. My intent was to point out that the people killed had not been innocent, and that their deaths had prevented many innocent children from being killed.

And not only had the abortionist been prevented from killing about thirty people that day, he had also been prevented from continuing to kill—unlike other abortionists who have merely been wounded and have returned to "work." The remarkable thing about that day was that the children survived to possibly work some other day, the one who intended to kill them did not.

At the police station, a specially summoned plain clothed officer sat talking with me for two or three hours. He had sat similarly with Michael Griffin. But I did not discuss what had just happened; I didn't want to aid those sworn to defend murder. It made little difference, however, since I had left an abundance of evidence, not intending to conceal my identity.

As I sat there talking, I was not sure whether I had been totally successful. Eventually the prosecutor came and declared with some flair, that he was charging me with two counts of murder. I then knew that I had accomplished my task. I continued to lift my heart to the Lord, thankful for success. I had not failed in my errand, and He had not failed me. The Lord had done great things through me.

A short time later, the arresting officer led me out of the police station, and escorted me twenty yards to his squad car in front of a teeming mass of reporters and photographers. As I came out of the door of the station, I seized the initiative, and raised my voice in a carefully planned declaration: "Now is the time to defend the unborn in the same way you'd defend slaves about to be murdered!"

Soon I was alone in a large one man cell, and could direct all my praise and thanks to the Lord. I repeatedly sang a song commonly used at rescues, "Our God is an Awesome God"; He is. The only way to handle the pain of being separated from my family was to continually rejoice in the Lord for all that He had done.

> *"By legalizing abortion, the government has aimed its intimidating weaponry at any who dare to interfere with the slaughter."*

Although I did not understand the meaning of all the emotions I experienced immediately after my incarceration, I understand them better now. Much of the joy I felt after shooting the abortionist, and still feel today, is the joy of having freely obeyed the Lord after being enslaved to fearful obedience to men.

I well remember (prior to the shooting) the oppressive feeling of realizing that I was not free to defend my neighbors as I would defend myself. Wrath was ready to be poured out on me if I cast off the shackles of passive submission to the state. The fear of being persecuted for disobeying our tyrannical government made submitting to its yoke seem attractive. My mind and will recoiled from the high cost of acting responsibly. It required an act of the will to even consider obeying the Lord.

Any nation that legalizes abortion throws a blanket of fear and intimidation over all its citizens who rightly understand the issues involved. By legalizing abortion, the government has aimed its intimidating weaponry at any who dare to interfere with the slaughter. The resulting fear of the government has a paralyzing effect on both the individual and the collective mindset that is incalculable. Anyone who underestimates the power that fear of the police has over men's minds fails to appreciate one of the government's most powerful tools. If you wonder why so few speak or practice the whole truth about defending the unborn you need look no further for an explanation; it's illegal to save those being led away to slaughter.

The inner joy and peace that has flooded my soul since I have cast off the state's tyranny makes my 6 x 9 cell a triumphant and newly liberated kingdom. I shudder at the thought of ever returning to the bondage currently enforced by the state.

> *"The focus should not be on the slain murderer, but on the deliverance of his intended victims."*

What is the appropriate and biblical response to news of an abortion provider being slain by someone defending the unborn? Under such circumstances, the focus should not be on the slain murderer, but on the deliverance of his intended victims. For instance, in the book of Esther, when the Lord delivered the Jews from the Persians that intended to harm them, the people didn't mourn the death of their enemies. Rather, they established a holiday of feasting and rejoicing that continues to be celebrated to this day.

Family Neglect and Excessive Force?

Many object that by acting as I did I have neglected my family. But in spite of the emphasis the Bible places on performing familial duties, it's abundantly clear that you must respond to the call of Christ—even if it requires you to leave your house, wife, children, and also forfeit your life. To perform a higher calling, it's often necessary to leave lesser duties behind.

Others object that killing Dr. Britton was excessive. But many who hold this position would not object if they learned that, during the Jewish holocaust, someone had shot and killed a Nazi concentration camp "doctor."

The appropriate degree of defensive force is determined by the circumstances.

Force which is excessive under one set of circumstances may be totally inadequate under conditions that are more demanding. Extreme circumstances normally call for extreme measures. Would you feel that you had done your duty if you merely wounded someone who was trying to kill your family, if, afterwards, you had to sit in jail as the murderer returned, week after week, until he had killed everyone in your family?

Under circumstances where it's likely that merely wounding someone, rather than killing him, will result in that person later returning to murder numerous people, lethal force

> *"Governments that sanction . . . mass murder should be resisted, and their innocent victims should be defended with the means necessary."*

is justified. Genesis 14 records an incident in which Abraham, and his men, attacked and killed a group of men who had taken Abraham's nephew, Lot, captive. God later blessed this slaughter through Melchizedek, who declared that God had delivered Abraham's enemies into his hand. Under these circumstances, lethal force was necessary. It certainly prevented those killed from later regrouping and returning to threaten Abraham or Lot.

Limited to Legal Remedies?

Many people mistakenly think that when the government sanctions mass murder that their responses should be limited to legal and educational remedies. But the appropriate response to an immediate threat to a child's life is not to merely pursue possible educational and legislative remedies, but to do what is necessary for the child's immediate and effective defense.

Those who believe that we should remain within the law, under these circumstances, have some difficult questions to answer. Would it also be wrong to intervene if the government was to sanction the murder of any other minority, and thousands were being slain in the streets every day? If individuals are wrong to bomb abortion clinics, would it have also been wrong for individuals to have bombed the tracks that led to Auschwitz?

If this is excessive, may Christians overturn the tables in abortion clinics, and chase everyone from the premises—much as Christ cleansed the temple? If not, why not? If mass rape or enslavement should be resisted with the immediate means necessary, should not mass murder be resisted with similar means?

Many people raise objections to my actions that can easily be resolved; many also refuse to take a definite stand on the weighty issues my actions raise. This is not, however, the way the Jews in the book of Esther, or Abraham, acted; if they had, the results would have been disastrous. They did not stagger at the duties laid before them, rather, they responded in faith—so should we.

A short time after my arrest, the prosecution announced they were seeking the death penalty. This forced me to decide whether I was going to resist their efforts to kill me. The threat of heightened persecution served to heighten my joy.

It was difficult for me to think of resisting something that would be such a great privilege.

After some thought, I decided that it was my duty to do whatever I could to save the most people from being killed. I didn't know for certain that my allowing them to kill me would result in fewer children being killed, but it seemed probable that this would be the result. I proceeded in the strength of this judgment.

Mock Trial

My trial was a classic example of judicial tyranny. It bore many similarities to the trials of those who protected the Jews from being murdered in Nazi Germany—prior to the end of the war. It should be remembered, however, that soon after the war many roles were reversed, and many who had sat in judgment on the defenders of the Jews were themselves judged.

With this in mind, Michael Hirsh, a pro-life lawyer formerly involved with *Operation Rescue,* presented a brief to the judge in my name. With the help of Vince Heiser (another pro-life lawyer who came to my aid) we argued that we should be allowed to show that my actions were necessary to prevent mass murder. We applied the principle of justifiable homicide to defending the unborn. We also reminded the judge that he might, one day, stand trial for upholding the abortion holocaust if he would not allow us to present the truth.

Even though 47% of the population believed that the abortionist was committing murder, the judge ruled against me, and would not allow me to voice this belief. He silenced me with a gag order.

The freedom to speak the truth—which every American should enjoy—was denied me during my trial. Even though my life hung in the balance, my pro-life views were strictly excluded by the court.

> *"Defending the unborn with force is considerably more than an idea whose time has come, it's a biblical duty whose time has come."*

If I had been allowed to tell the truth, it would have inevitably resulted in my putting the abortionist, and the government which protected him, on trial for participating in mass murder. I could have shown that not only the abortionist, but also the government, could have justifiably had force used against it. Governments that sanction and enforce mass murder should be resisted, and their innocent victims should be defended with the means necessary.

Since I was denied a truthful defense, I had none. What was I to say? Since I could not tell the truth, I had almost nothing to say. There was no use in offering lame and ineffectual arguments—doing so would only make it appear that I had been given a fair trial.

During the penalty phase, I addressed the jury for the first time, and made a short statement as my "closing argument":

You have a responsibility to protect your neighbor's life, and to use force if necessary to do so. In an effort to suppress this truth, you may mix my blood with the blood of the unborn, and those who have fought to defend the oppressed. However, truth and righteousness will prevail. May God help you to protect the unborn as you would want to be protected.

Soon afterwards, I was escorted to Florida State Prison's death row.

I could not avoid an automatic appeal to the Florida State Supreme Court. As soon as they upheld my death sentence, I waived all future appeals.

World-Transforming Truths

The most powerful weapon for overcoming the world's apathetic response to legal abortion is to advocate the means necessary for resisting this atrocity (as required by God's law). Neither the world nor the worldly Christian want the searchlight of God's Word focused on their neglect of the unborn, but these are the means God uses to produce genuine repentance.

Without a lofty ethic there can be no hearty repentance; without a sight of sin there is no need of a Savior. How can you expect to convict people of neglecting the unborn, and point them to Christ for pardon, unless the requirements of God's law are being applied to the abortion holocaust?

God's arm is not short. If only a few show the commitment required, He can turn the tide on legalized abortion and begin a worldwide transformation. Victor Hugo has written, "One can resist an invasion of armies, but not an idea whose time has come." Defending the unborn with force is considerably more than an idea whose time has come, it's a biblical duty whose time has come.

God is able to bless the application of this duty exceedingly abundantly beyond all we could ask or think. If Christians will take a bold stand on this duty, regardless of the cost, the Lord will fight for us, and win a great victory for His own glory and honor. If, therefore, you believe that abortion is lethal force you should uphold the force needed to stop it.

Laws Restricting Protests Are Unjust

by Steven T. McFarland

About the author: *Steven T. McFarland is a lawyer and the director of the Christian Legal Society's Center for Law and Religious Freedom in Annandale, Virginia.*

With so many abortion-rights activists in the Clinton administration, it should be no surprise that the United States government has turned up the heat against the pro-life movement. The Freedom of Access to Clinic Entrances (FACE) Act of 1994 may force all but the most courageous to keep their pro-life opinions to themselves, raising serious questions about this administration's regard for the First Amendment.

On the surface, FACE looks good. It is being sold as an effort to control the most outrageous acts committed in the name of the pro-life movement. Yet this plainly is not the act's primary purpose, and it certainly will not be its sole effect. With rare exceptions, states were already adequately prosecuting crimes committed against abortionists. Furthermore, the act itself is not limited to such extreme cases. The shooting of abortionists in Florida and Kansas provided the necessary political cover for a far more ambitious project to silence by intimidation all but the bravest in the pro-life movement.

Overly Broad Restrictions

Supporters of FACE will respond that it has nothing to do with free speech—that it targets only the more extreme and violent tactics used by some elements of the pro-life movement. Yet the wording of the new statute (despite some improvement over earlier versions) permits its application to a broad array of situations far removed from its alleged focus.

FACE promises severe criminal penalties and civil liability judgments against anyone who (by force, threat of force, or physical obstruction) "intentionally injures, intimidates, or interferes" with someone obtaining or providing an abortion. Just about anything a pro-life protester might do on a sidewalk outside an

Reprinted from Steven T. McFarland, "Pro-Lifers' New Legal Nightmare," *Christianity Today*, August 15, 1994. Reprinted with permission from the author.

abortion clinic could be construed as violating the act. Carrying a sign, trying to talk to a would-be patient or clinic worker, or even kneeling or pausing for prayer could "interfere" by "physical obstruction." To convict or impose liability, a judge need only believe that the presence of a protest makes it "unreasonably difficult" to enter or leave the abortion clinic. Similarly, the very sight of protest is inherently intimidating for some. If the presence of peaceful demonstrators is emotionally disturbing to a patient inside the clinic, her mental distress could be sufficient "intentional injury" on which to sue the protesters under the act.

> *"Just about anything a pro-life protester might do . . . outside an abortion clinic could be construed as violating the [law]."*

Just as numerous as the potential violations are the potential "victims" and crime sites under the act. The crime need not occur at the abortion clinic, and the complainant need not be an abortion worker or patient in order for federal or state authorities to be called in—facts that might surprise those who voted for FACE in Congress. For example, authorities could seek a gag order against a pastor whose sermon advocates peaceful blocking of access to an abortion clinic, because the message might intimidate someone who is thinking about going to a clinic.

Unfair Punishment

The act's drafters apparently recognized that some "victims" bringing such lawsuits would not be able to demonstrate that they suffered legally recognizable harm. So Congress declared that litigants could recover $5,000 in compensation without even having to prove that they suffered actual damages. Moreover, FACE allows juries to punish protesters by imposing huge, punitive damage awards. Congress also reversed the normal presumption that each side pay his or her own attorney's fees, imposing the obligation for costs and fees upon a losing defendant. However, a successful defendant can recover her fees only if she can demonstrate that the plaintiff's suit was utterly frivolous, which is virtually impossible to do. This is a plaintiff lawyer's paradise.

Finally, the act also grants draconian powers to the Justice Department. A first-time offender can get up to a year in prison and a $10,000 fine; if anyone is injured (for example, from a scuffle with pro-choice counter-demonstrators), the sentence can go up to ten years.

Regulating Free Speech

When the government seeks to regulate free speech protected by the First Amendment—which includes a pro-life protest—courts require that the law's wording be highly precise. Vagueness of the kind permeating FACE presents three major dangers: lack of fair notice of what is prohibited; a chilling effect on free speech; the risk of discriminatory enforcement against an unpopular viewpoint. This creates ideal conditions for the government to suppress politically incorrect speech in public.

The FACE Act raises the stakes in abortion protest, muting by self-censorship America's prophetic voices of protest. To prevent this tragedy, the law must be challenged in court until free speech is vindicated or Congress realizes what it hath wrought.

Violence Against Abortion Clinics Is Not Justifiable

by Mary Lou Greenberg

About the author: *Mary Lou Greenberg, the managing editor of* On the Issues *magazine, is an abortion rights activist who has defended clinics and worked with abortion providers nationwide.*

As I held in my hand the sharp slivers of glass that were now the only remains of the shattered windows, my eye was drawn to a metal object in the debris. It was a nail, a small, sharp spike two inches long. I shuddered. Hundreds of these projectiles intended to shred human flesh had been propelled outward by the blast when the bomb went off, just a few feet from the main entrance. I could still see some of the nails embedded in the building's masonry facade, between the now boarded-up door and bits of what had been an awning. A crater, a foot deep, marked where the bomb had been planted. The trajectory of the nails and shrapnel was toward the front door and windows, and the reception area just inside. If the bomb had gone off minutes later, women coming to the clinic for abortions would have been among its victims. As it was, security guard Robert D. Sanderson was killed in the explosion, and nurse Emily Lyons was severely injured. The bomb was not meant to destroy the building—the New Woman All Women Health Care clinic in Birmingham, Alabama, sustained no structural damage—but the walls of the reception area were torn by the nails.

Just as this anti-personnel bomb at the clinic was intended to rip apart bodies, so too was it meant to penetrate people's minds and emotions with a chilling message: If you provide abortions, if you work at clinics or go to them as clients, you will be a target! This is the stark reality behind the statistics on clinic violence: Between 1993 and 1998, six people were assassinated at five clinics. They included two doctors, two clinic workers, one clinic escort, and the security guard in Birmingham. Seven others were wounded in these attacks. During the same period, two more doctors were seriously injured—one was shot, the other slashed with a knife—outside their clinics. And three physicians were shot and

Excerpted from Mary Lou Greenberg, "The Fire This Time," *On the Issues*, Summer 1998. Reprinted with permission from *On the Issues*.

wounded by a sniper or snipers in Canada. In 1997, there were a total of 12 bombings or arsons at U.S. clinics, the highest annual rate since 1984.

I have traveled to the sites of all the fatal anti-abortion assaults to help organize pro-choice demonstrations against the attacks and to support the clinics. Now, in Birmingham, these bomb shards brought home to me once again, with vivid, gut-wrenching intensity, the seriousness and viciousness of this war.

But as soon as the yellow crime-scene tape came down, and clinic staff were allowed to enter the building, an outpouring of support and assistance both locally and across the country turned the intended message of intimidation on its head. It was hard for some of the local people to approach the building; images of their absent colleagues, recurring in news photos, were vivid in their minds. But as volunteers began to sweep up the glass inside and out, and the clinic's owner, Diane Derzis, and its administrator, Michelle Farley, made plans for repairs, the work at hand propelled all of us forward. Workers were soon filling the holes and repainting the walls, and installing new glass. A shredded sofa was removed from the reception room, and chairs from an inside room which had not been damaged were brought out to replace it. New plants were delivered. And the phone began ringing with calls from women who wanted to make appointments.

"This Clinic Stays Open!"

At an outdoor press conference exactly one week after the bombing, Jeff Lyons, the 41-year-old husband of the injured nurse, spoke for us all. "I just want to tell whoever did this," he said defiantly, pointing to the clinic, "it didn't work!" Diane Derzis announced proudly that the clinic was open again, and with a full staff—there had not been one resignation, and another nurse had come forward to fill in for Emily Lyons. A sign in the window boldly proclaimed: "This clinic stays open!"

In the weeks to come, Emily's continuing recovery and courage would be an inspiration to everyone. The nurse lost her left eye and sustained serious injuries to her right one; she had multiple shrapnel wounds in her face and torso, a broken left leg, and damage to the muscle in her right leg and to both shins. She was forced to undergo numerous surgical procedures, and received intensive physical therapy. Yet this mother of two teenage daughters by a previous marriage is hopeful of walking, even jogging, again. In a statement read by her husband at a press conference, she said the bombing had not swayed her from her strong belief that women should have the right to an abortion if they choose. "Abortion is a legal and legitimate form of health care, and I offer no apologies for being employed there," she said.

> *"If the bomb had gone off minutes later, women coming to the clinic for abortions would have been among its victims."*

Chapter 4

Pro-Choice vs. Pro-Life

I arrived in Birmingham on Friday, January 30, the day after the bombing. On Saturday morning, I and other out-of-town activists from Refuse & Resist! (an organization formed in 1988 to oppose today's repressive political agenda) went to Summit Medical Center, another abortion clinic just a block away, to join local volunteers in escorting clients to the clinic. When we arrived, there was a small crowd at the entrance to the driveway. Some wore neon-orange vests with "clinic escort" printed on the front in bold, black letters, and were waving cars into the parking lot. But local anti-abortion activists were present, too. Showing no remorse about the fatal bombing the day before, they thrust signs with anti-abortion slogans at the occupants of the cars and yelled, "Don't murder your baby!" The demonstration was being orchestrated by the national leader of Operation Rescue National, Flip Benham. Well-tanned, and with a TV evangelist's perpetual smile, Benham, like a military commander, could be heard urging his troops to give their all.

One man, who had driven a woman to her appointment at the clinic, stormed across the sidewalk to confront the protesters, with their photos of what they claimed were bloody aborted fetuses. "The bombing was terrible. Why are you out here?" he demanded. A protester wearing a clerical collar pointed to the poster of a fetus and began to speak, but the challenger cut him off: "This is about a woman's life," he said, gesturing toward the clinic door. "It's her choice. Not yours!" A woman holding

> *"Bomb shards brought home . . . with vivid, gut-wrenching intensity, the seriousness and viciousness of this war."*

anti-abortion pamphlets tried to elbow me away from the clinic driveway. I asked her how she felt about the death and injuries caused by the bombing. She muttered that she was "sorry" about the security guard, but sorrier about "the babies being murdered." Other anti-abortion protesters echoed this sentiment. One man, who had been at the bomb scene shortly after the explosion, told the *Birmingham News:* "I don't like to see anybody die, but they're in a business of death. . . . You live by the sword, you die by the sword. We've told them that they're in a grisly business—the flesh trade. You never know what's going to happen to you. . . . There are 200 to 300 people [sic] killed a week in those clinics. That's a much more tragic loss of life."

Such rhetoric encourages attacks on clinics and staff, says David Gunn Jr., son of Dr. David Gunn, who was murdered outside a Pensacola, Florida, clinic in 1993—the first physician killed by an anti-abortion gunman. As long as anti-abortion demonstrators continue to call clinic workers "murderers," he said, "you can't be surprised" by such attacks.

Justifying the "pro-life" activists' kill-people campaign, Rev. Donald Spitz, director of Pro-Life Virginia, sent an e-mail to a columnist for the *Birmingham Post-Herald,* stating: "Robert Sanderson [the security guard] was the protector of the baby killers and was an accessory to murder. He was paid with blood money from the babies that were slaughtered. He reaped what he sowed. He was not a hero or a good person. He was a killer, an accessory to murder. He deserved exactly what he received."

Spitz also intruded on the website Emily Lyons' husband set up to enable people to send their get-well wishes to Emily and to publish updates on the progress of her recovery. Addressing himself to the wounded nurse, Spitz wrote: "Emily, there are many, many people who believe you reaped what you sowed. I am one of them. I hope you get out of the BABYKILLING business. Your husband is going around showing your picture for sympathy. He doesn't show any pictures of the babies you helped murder. Why not?"

> *"Local anti-abortion activists were present, . . . showing no remorse about the fatal bombing the day before."*

The national media gave a platform to others to promote the same message. Michael Bray, who served four years in jail for a string of clinic bombings in the Washington, D.C., area, told a nationwide audience on ABC-TV's *Nightline* that he had no misgivings about the clinic bombing, "given the benefit that comes from it and the issues at stake." Bray also praised the Army of God, which had claimed credit for the 1997 bombings of an abortion clinic and a lesbian-owned nightclub in Atlanta, as well as the Birmingham bombing.

On the surface, claiming to be "pro-life" yet approving cold-blooded murder reflects either twisted logic or rank hypocrisy. But such words provide moral justification and encouragement for those who plant the bombs and pull the triggers.

Such justification also indicates that the movement's real agenda is not the protection of so-called unborn "people," but a political campaign bent on denying women, at any cost, the right to decide how their lives will be lived.

Nationwide Harassment

Anti-abortion campaigners' comments to the media cannot be dismissed as the rantings of lone crazies. They must be seen for what they are: rallying cries for the brutal, storm-trooper wing of the anti-abortion movement, a movement that is funded and sustained by powerful, well-organized, well-connected forces hiding behind professedly moral motivations.

A number of the Birmingham-based anti-abortion protesters are part of a committed national movement that has harassed abortion providers and clinic clients across the country. I had seen their faces in Dayton, Ohio, in July 1997, when they helped Operation Rescue (OR) blockade and close clinics there. Outside the clinics, OR leaders preached and testified about the "glories" of women submitting to men. And on January 22, 1998, the 25th anniversary of *Roe v. Wade,* these same people were present in front of the Supreme Court, where they participated in a large anti-abortion march. They were the thugs who bullied and shoved pro-choice demonstrators on the steps of the Court, as we held up a large banner that read, "They can't have our day, or our lives!" The Reverend Spitz was there, too, holding a sign reading: "Free Paul Hill— Execute Abortionists." Hill is the man convicted of killing Dr. James Bayard Britton and clinic escort James Barrett, in Pensacola, in 1994.

Such zealots are unyielding in their determination to intimidate women and abortion providers and, ultimately, to halt abortion entirely. "If you don't want to be pregnant, keep your legs closed!" snarled one man to a young pro-choice woman at the Supreme Court.

But there is committed determination on the pro-choice side, too, as exemplified by the courage and dedication of the clinic employees and escorts in Birmingham. They had been seasoned over a period of a dozen years, dealing with anti-abortion protesters who have continually targeted both the Summit and the New Woman clinics. Many clinic employees and escorts live near the clinic, so when the bomb exploded they knew immediately what had happened. People promptly began mobilizing, and grief quickly turned to resolve as volunteers started calling the Birmingham Clinic Defense Team's hotline to see what they could do. Some local people who had not been involved before offered to be escorts. Others stepped up their activism because, as one said, "Women can't be truly equal until they can control their bodies. I've decided that this fight is mine as long as it takes.". . .

Drawing the Line in Birmingham

The Birmingham bombing was part of a many-pronged attack on abortion rights and access. The response to the attack, however, indicates that we may be moving toward a new level of national unity and support for the providers who make "choice" possible. . . .

Today, new sod has replaced the shards of glass which covered the lawn of the Birmingham clinic after the bombing. A new maroon awning with crisp white lettering shades the doorway. And a new level of energy and determination to defend abortion access and women's lives is coming out of the horror of that early morning in January.

Laws Restricting Protests Are Just

by Fay Clayton and Sara N. Love

About the authors: *Fay Clayton is a partner with the Chicago-based law firm Robinson, Curley, and Clayton; Sara N. Love is the attorney for the National Women's Health Foundation in Washington, D.C. Clayton and Love represented the plaintiff in* NOW v. Scheidler.

In *Roe v. Wade,* the United States Supreme Court held that women have a constitutional right to choose to have an abortion. Yet, since shortly after *Roe,* women have often found themselves unable to exercise that right because of forcible and violent interference by abortion opponents. In March 1998, the National Organization for Women (NOW) and two women's health clinics that provide abortions went to trial in *NOW v. Scheidler* to ensure that the constitutional right recognized twenty-five years earlier would exist not just in theory, but in reality. After a seven-week trial, the federal jury found each of the defendants liable for 121 predicate (criminal) acts under the Racketeer Influenced and Corrupt Organizations Act (RICO).

NOW v. Scheidler was filed in federal court in 1986. The case was brought by NOW, the Delaware Women's Health Organization (DWHO), and the Summit Women's Health Organization ("Summit") against Joseph Scheidler; Randall Terry; Andrew Scholberg; Timothy Murphy; the Pro-Life Action League, Inc. ("Scheidler's organization"); and Operation Rescue ("Terry's organization") for violations of the racketeering laws by operating an enterprise—the Pro-Life Action Network (PLAN)—through a pattern of criminal acts. . . .

The Climate of Terrorism in the Early 1980s

While *Roe v. Wade* guaranteed women the right to choose to have an abortion, even after *Roe,* women's health clinics that provide abortions, together with their volunteers, staff, and patients, continued to encounter enormous difficulties exercising that right, due to physical interference from abortion foes. By the early 1980s, antiabortion extremists had embarked on a campaign of

Excerpted from Fay Clayton and Sara N. Love, *"NOW v. Scheidler:* Protecting Women's Access to Reproductive Health Services," *Albany Law Review*, Spring 1999. Reprinted with permission from *Albany Law Review.*

terrorism designed to chill the exercise of this constitutional right. They vowed to stop at nothing to prevent abortions from being performed, and their tactics ranged from forcible harassment, like shoving patients and staff and blocking entrances, to the most violent of crimes, such as bombings, arson, and kidnappings. In 1986, after futile attempts to persuade President Ronald Reagan and his Attorney General to take steps to end the violence, NOW and two clinics decided to fight back. Realizing the need for a nationwide remedy against anti-abortion extremists, these plaintiffs brought a national class-action lawsuit in federal court against Joseph Scheidler and the other key leaders and organizations. This suit was both brave and novel. It was brave because it was brought against terrorists by those they had terrorized. It was novel because it was a new use of the racketeering laws, and it was the first such case brought as a class action.

Because PLAN's campaign of terrorism had been launched against every woman who sought an abortion and every clinic in the country that offered them, NOW brought the case for both its members and the class of all women who had used or would use the clinics; and the clinics brought the case for the class of all women's health clinics in the continental United States that provided abortion services.

Since *Roe,* anti-choice forces had tried a variety of tactics to make clinics and women give up their rights to provide or receive abortions, but by the early 1980s, the tactics had turned truly ugly. Glue was poured into door locks, and clinics were bombed, set on fire, and polluted with butyric acid. While the tactics varied, the goals were the same: to shut down the clinics so women could not receive any medical services there and to force the clinics to stop performing abortions. Although the class of clinics provided a full range of women's health services from general gynecology and birth control to abortion, Scheidler, Terry, and their followers targeted the clinics as "abortion mills" in their efforts to marginalize them and incite acts of violence against them.

Abortion opponents who protested outside the clinics ran the gamut from lawful protesters who prayed, sang, and passed out leaflets, to lawful but obnoxious protesters who screamed "murderer" and "baby-killer," to outright thugs who physically assaulted the women and the clinic escorts and barricaded the doors. While the first two types of protests are, of course, protected by the First Amendment,

> *"By the early 1980s, anti-abortion extremists had embarked on a campaign of terrorism."*

the third is not. But the limits of the law made no difference to Scheidler and his followers, who declared themselves above the law, and who wove obtuse arguments about how their end justified their means. Answering only to what they called "higher laws," PLAN activists used whatever tools of force and violence they found effective. Scheidler declared that he would "never" follow the law of the land and urged his growing band of followers to "stop abortion in every way possible."

The women who used the clinics were harassed regardless of the reason for their visit, as the evidence at trial would demonstrate. Even if they were merely seeking annual physicals, contraceptives, or cancer screening, they were threatened, attacked, shoved, and grabbed. NOW members and others who volunteered as escorts to shield the patients were subjected to the same brutal harassment.

> *"[Pro-lifers] targeted the clinics as 'abortion mills' in their efforts to marginalize them and incite acts of violence against them."*

Some of the extremists' worst tactics were saved for doctors and other clinic staff. They stalked them, threatened their lives and those of their families, and damaged or destroyed their cars and other property. They even printed and distributed "wanted" posters detailing where they lived, descriptions of their cars and the routes they took to work, and the names, ages, and schools of family members. The terrorism was not isolated: it happened across the entire country, and it happened in remarkably similar ways—it was not only relentless but highly organized.

It was in this climate of terrorism that NOW, Summit, and DWHO brought their case.

RICO: Tailor-Made for *Scheidler*

The Racketeer Influenced and Corrupt Organizations Act (RICO), prohibits those engaged in an interstate "enterprise" from conducting the affairs of that enterprise through "a pattern of racketeering activity." RICO allows either a government prosecutor or private plaintiffs who have been injured in their business or property to hold the leaders of the "enterprise" responsible for the criminal acts of its foot soldiers. Even if those who operate the enterprise keep their hands clean and avoid personal liability for the underlying illegal ("predicate") acts, they may be held responsible under RICO for operating the enterprise through a pattern of that illegal conduct.

The elements of a RICO violation are straightforward. First, . . . there must be an enterprise, which can be any type of entity, whether a formal, legal organization, like a corporation, or an informal association-in-fact, such as a coalition of anti-abortion groups. The enterprise need not be an illegal organization in itself; it is enough that it carries out illegal acts along with some lawful ones. The enterprise must have some structure, although not much is required. Second, the defendant must be associated with the enterprise and must operate or manage it. Third, the enterprise must affect interstate commerce. Fourth, the enterprise must be conducted through a "pattern of racketeering activity." Racketeering activity includes any act or threat involving several enumerated state-law felonies or any act that is punishable under several enumerated federal statutes.

These enumerated crimes are called acts of "racketeering" or "predicate acts." RICO's "pattern" requirement calls for some continuity among the predicate acts, although it may be satisfied by as few as two related acts within a ten-year period. These elements fit the defendants' conduct like a glove, as the jury in *Scheidler* would conclude.

The Pro-Life Mafia

Among the most visible anti-abortion leaders in the mid-1980s were Joseph Scheidler, Andrew Scholberg, Timothy Murphy, Randall Terry, and their organizations, the Pro-Life Action League, Inc., and Operation Rescue. In 1984, Joseph Scheidler, Andrew Scholberg, and a handful of other self-described "radical" antiabortion leaders formed a loosely organized coalition that they named PLAN—the Pro-Life Action Network. PLAN was a nationwide organization of anti-abortion groups that got together to plan ways to intimidate clinics so that they would stop offering abortions. PLAN functioned largely through annual conventions held in cities all across the country, with private sessions for "known radicals" only. The individual defendants rarely missed a PLAN meeting, and they often played organizational roles in planning them, setting their agendas, and organizing field training to teach new ways to interfere with clinic operations. PLAN also had a Leadership Council that met at irregular intervals between the annual conventions. At these meetings, the Leadership Council members assigned tasks such as networking, fund raising, handling public relations, and developing new tactics. It was a classic RICO "enterprise."

PLAN operated much like the Mafia. In fact, in early correspondence, Scheidler called PLAN the "pro-life mafia." Tellingly, mainstream groups like the National Right-to-Life Committee, which was pledged to oppose abortion through lawful means, were not invited to participate. Instead, PLAN took its inspiration from felons who had committed violent crimes, like bombings, arson, and kidnapping of doctors. Scheidler praised these convicted criminals for their effectiveness and their zeal, and encouraged and condoned violent acts.

> *"The terrorism was not isolated: it happened in remarkably similar ways—it was not only relentless but highly organized."*

Not totally unmindful of the lawsuits he might face, Scheidler paid lip-service to non-violence, but then he would speak out of the other side of his mouth and announce that arson isn't violence because it only destroys "bricks and glass"!

The early leaders of PLAN set up their enterprise in such a way that the criminal acts were typically planned and orchestrated at secret sessions to which only those with proven criminal records for anti-abortion activity were invited. When the crimes were carried out, PLAN's leaders would usually be far enough away that they were unlikely to be arrested. The behind-the-scenes roles that the defendants played in PLAN easily satisfied the association and management elements of RICO.

Because PLAN's conventions and the accompanying attacks on clinics were held in various states across the country, the enterprise unquestionably affected interstate commerce. PLAN's members traveled from all parts of the country to attend the conventions and to learn and practice PLAN's latest illegal methods. In addition, the clinics made substantial purchases of goods and services in interstate commerce—purchases that were impacted by PLAN's blockades. PLAN's use of the mails, phone lines, and various modes of interstate transportation was extensive and readily satisfied RICO's interstate commerce requirement.

> *"From the beginning, the case [against anti-abortion protesters] was based upon acts of force and violence, not speech or advocacy."*

Attacks on DWHO and the Ladies' Center

Finally, while RICO requires a minimum of two related predicate acts, from its formation in 1984 until the trial in 1998, the defendants conducted PLAN through a pattern of hundreds, if not thousands, of these acts. Two early examples—in fact the two incidents that led the plaintiffs to file this lawsuit—were committed against the original lead plaintiff clinics, DWHO and the Ladies' Center.

In April 1986, shortly after several clinics had been bombed, Scheidler and three other large, burly PLAN activists paid a visit on DWHO. The clinic administrator—a petite, young woman—was there alone, and the intruders positioned themselves in such a way that they prevented her escape. She asked them to leave, but they refused. One of these men reached over the reception desk, commandeered the telephones and put them on hold, effectively cutting the clinic administrator off from the outside world. Once they had her trapped, they warned her that they were there to "case the place," to make "Delaware . . . the first abortion-free state in the nation," and that she had better leave her job.

The other incident occurred in March 1986. Scheidler and John Ryan flew to Pensacola to meet with John Butt, Joan Andrews, and several other PLAN leaders. (Andrews had already achieved fame by invading clinics and destroying equipment.) They made plans for an invasion of the Ladies' Center the following day. Butt and Andrews promised to be among the invaders, and Scheidler agreed that he might enter the clinic too—if he could get away without being arrested. The next day, while Scheidler limited his role to "public relations" on the street, Butt, Andrews, and a number of other PLAN activists burst into the clinic, pushed the administrator down the stairs and slammed the NOW escort up against the wall, causing them both serious injuries. The invaders then proceeded to destroy the Ladies' Center's medical equipment. Afterwards, Scheidler bragged about the invasion and took credit for it, saying that he had "shut down an abortuary for a couple of days.". . .

NOW v. Scheidler and the First Amendment

It took twelve years for *NOW v. Scheidler* to come to trial. The two main factors that contributed to the length of that period were a trip to the Supreme Court and defendants' continuing efforts to delay their day of judgment. . . .

From the beginning of *NOW v. Scheidler,* the defendants and their supporters had tried to invoke the First Amendment as a shield for their acts of force and violence. They argued essentially that if speech is an element of their acts of brutality, the First Amendment immunizes those acts. Needless to say, they have never been able to cite any authority for such a proposition, since well-settled Supreme Court case law holds to the contrary.

It was clear to the jury that *NOW v. Scheidler* was not about protected speech. From the outset of the case, NOW and the clinics were careful to avoid challenging any anti-abortion protests that did not involve force or violence. As an advocacy organization itself, NOW is keenly aware of the role that speech plays in our nation's culture; but as NOW has often noted, there is a major difference between non-violent civil disobedience, like that advocated by Dr. Martin Luther King, Jr., and the kind of non-civil violent disobedience in which the PLAN defendants engaged. . . .

> *"The First Amendment does not protect those who use speech to plot and organize criminal acts."*

Picketing, leafleting, and other forms of advocacy—the classic tools of social protest movements—were never a part of the Scheidler case. The plaintiffs never claimed that speech, even the ugly speech that the defendants used—calling the patients, staff and volunteers "murderers," and "baby killers,"—was a RICO violation. The plaintiffs recognized that unpleasant speech is an important part of the free speech protected by the First Amendment. . . . From the beginning, the case was based upon acts of force and violence, not speech or advocacy. It was only because PLAN gave up on speech and adopted violence as its chief weapon that NOW brought this lawsuit. . . .

Many of PLAN's leaders (some of whom were active in the Ku Klux Klan in earlier years) tried to take advantage of the case law established by the civil rights protesters. But rather than relying on the power of a peaceful march or a well-spoken message, PLAN's true role model was the segregation opponents . . . blockading students at the schoolhouse door. Rather than teaching supporters to be prayerful and to turn the other cheek, as Dr. Martin Luther King did, PLAN taught its foot soldiers to use kryptonite locks, massive blockades and to "stop abortion in every way possible." PLAN ridiculed those who relied on letters to the editors, lobbying, and other forms of protected speech, calling them "wimps."

PLAN's chief tools were violence and the overt threat of further violence. PLAN abandoned speech in favor of force and threats of force. It was entirely appropriate that RICO—a law originally designed to combat the mafia—has been used to combat the criminal anti-abortion mafia known as "PLAN."

Chapter 5

Should Aborted Fetuses Be Used for Medical Research?

Chapter Preface

Despite being hailed as a scientific breakthrough in treating debilitating diseases, transplants using fetal tissue remain a controversial area of research due to the tissue's source—aborted fetuses. Embryonic stem cells from fetuses have the potential to grow into a variety of body parts and organs, including the heart, brain, and nervous system. Scientists hope that transplanting these fundamental stem cells will help regenerate diseased cells, offering an effective treatment and possible cure for such diseases as Parkinson's and Alzheimer's.

During the late 1980s and 1990s, many scientists focused their fetal tissue research on the treatment of Parkinson's disease. Advocates of fetal tissue transplants have praised the results of clinical trials that injected fetal brain tissue deep into the deteriorating brains of Parkinson's sufferers. They assert that, unlike transplants involving adult tissue, fetal tissue transplants appear to grow and flourish in their new environment, reinvigorating the brain with much-needed chemicals. According to journalist Tracy Watson, "In some of the several dozen Parkinson's patients who have had fetal nerve cells implanted in their failing brains . . . , the improvement has been spectacular." A number of Parkinson's patients who participated in similar clinical studies have also reported improvement in their overall well-being, movement, and muscle flexibility.

Many medical researchers, however, question the scientific merits and medical benefits of fetal tissue transplants. These critics argue that Parkinson's experiments involving fetal tissue transplants have yielded only mediocre results and have failed to show functional improvement in patients with the worst cases of the disease. Furthermore, they suggest that the improvements reported by patients who have undergone fetal tissue transplants are nothing more than a placebo effect—an improvement triggered by the mental rather than physical aspects of the treatment. Opponents of fetal tissue research propose abandoning this line of research altogether and pursuing more therapeutic alternatives. These research options include stem cell stimulation, in which dormant embryonic stem cells in an adult's brain can be stimulated to allow the brain to regenerate itself; pallidotomy, which involves surgically applying microscopic lesions to the globus pallidus, an area deep within the brain, to improve muscle function; and brain pacemakers, which would provide constant stimulation. Until additional trials are conducted and the procedure's long-term effects can be evaluated, the debate over the medical potential of fetal tissue transplants is likely to continue. In the following chapter, doctors, scientists, and ethicists address this issue and others as they examine whether tissue derived from aborted fetuses should be used in medical research.

Fetal Tissue Research Will Benefit Medical Science

by Dorothy C. Wertz

About the author: *Social scientist and ethicist Dorothy C. Wertz is coediter of the* Gene Letter, *an electronic newsletter that focuses on genetics, ethics, and public policy.*

Scientists have isolated and grown embryonic cells that are capable of becoming many different organs, if given the proper genetic directions. On November 6, 1998, the *New York Times* reported that two groups of researchers, one headed by Dr. James A. Thomson of the University of Wisconsin, Madison, and the other by Dr. John Gearhart of Johns Hopkins University, Baltimore, had succeeded in growing human stem cells in the laboratory. The hope is that these could be used to grow organs for transplantation. Since the Federal Government has consistently refused to support research on the human embryo or embryonic cells, both projects were funded by Geron Corporation of Menlo Park, CA, a biotechnology company that specializes in genetic research on aging.

The two teams of researchers used different methods to isolate stem cells. Dr. Thomson's cells were taken from a 15- to 20-cell "pre-embryo" called a blastocyst, about three days after fertilization. At this point in development, each cell is "pluripotent," meaning that it has the power to become many different parts of the body. (The stem cells may even be "totipotent," meaning that they can become all organs in the body, but this has not been demonstrated.) About half the cells in a blastocyst become the placenta; the rest eventually become part of a developing embryo, at about 14 days. At the blastocyst stage, however, all the cells are the same; there is no way of knowing whether a particular cell will become embryo or placenta. Once the embryo becomes differentiated from the placenta, however, the stem cells start to become specialized into those that become heart, liver, spine, nervous system, etc. and lose their potentiality to become anything else.

Dr. Gearhart's group isolated its stem cells from the germ cells (precursors of

Excerpted from Dorothy C. Wertz, "Human Embryonic Stem Cells: A Source of Organ Transplants," *Gene Letter*, February 1999. Reprinted with permission from the author.

eggs and sperm) of aborted fetuses. Germ cells, unlike other cells in the developing fetus, are not committed to developing into particular organs. They remain pluripotent, in order to carry their genetic information forward in the next generation. Stem cells taken from the germ cells of a fetus may be equivalent to stem cells taken from a blastocyst, but this remains to be proven.

Stem cells are immortal and can be grown indefinitely in the laboratory. Cells only become mortal—losing their ability to grow and divide indefinitely—after they become specialized.

Researchers hope that they will be able to direct stem cells to form organs for transplantation. At this point, no one knows how to do this, so transplantable organs may be a long way off. Experiments with mouse stem cells show that if injected into an organ of another mouse, for example, the heart, the stem cells specialize into cells for that organ, but this is not the same as growing an entire heart for transplantation and may not even be medically useful.

Although isolating stem cells is a breakthrough, the next step—developing the directions to program them—could take many years. Even if it becomes possible to grow entire organs, problems of rejection by the body's immune system may remain.

Ethical Issues

Just about anything with the label "embryo" or "fetus" arouses many people's concerns about the dignity of human life or human potential. It is important to remember that a three-day-old blastocyst is not yet even an embryo. Any particular cell is as likely to become part of the placenta, which will be discarded at birth, as it is to become part of a "potential person." Ethics commissions in several nations, including Australia, the United Kingdom (the Warnock Report), the United States (National Institutes of Health Human Embryo Research Panel, 1994), and, more recently, Denmark, have approved research on the human embryo up to 14 days. Up to 14 days, it is more properly called a "pre-embryo," because the embryo is not differentiated from other tissue. At 14 days, a structure called the "primitive streak" appears, which will become the brain and spinal column and which differentiates embryo from placenta. Before 14 days, there is no possibility of pain or sentience and no cells that will definitely become part of an individual.

> *"Research on embryos and fetuses that would otherwise be thrown away . . . dignifies life by perhaps helping to save others."*

The NIH panel, unlike the Warnock Report, approved creation of pre-embryos specifically for research if there were not enough "surplus" pre-embryos donated after IVF [in vitro fertilization]. Many members of the U.S. public objected, and Congress instituted a ban on federal funds for embryo research in 1995, continuing an over 20-year history of refusal of federal support. Thus, virtually all research on human reproduction and infertility, including IVF, has been financed by the private sector. Pre-embryos not used in IVF are sometimes donated for research with informed consent by the couple. These pre-embryos will never be implanted in a woman's uterus and would otherwise be discarded after about two or three years.

The proposed new research does not depend upon continued use of pre-embryos. Once cells have been isolated from a blastocyst, they can grow and divide indefinitely in the laboratory, so new blastocysts are not necessary.

Legal Issues

On January 19, 1999, the Department of Health and Human Services ruled that embryonic stem cells do not fall under the 1995 Congressional ban on embryo research. NIH is therefore legally free to fund initial derivation of these cells from an embryo.

Use of germ cells taken from aborted fetuses (the Johns Hopkins group) may be more problematic ethically. Nevertheless, it is important to remember that research on already aborted fetuses does not cause women to have abortions. Requests for donations are made only after the woman has decided upon abortion, and she receives no compensation for the donation. To say that fetal research causes abortions is a bit like saying that a need for donor organs causes murders. Research on embryos and fetuses that would otherwise be thrown away does not cause indignity to human life. On the contrary, it dignifies life by perhaps helping to save others.

> *"Growing organs from human embryonic stem cells could . . . save thousands of lives a year."*

Need for Organs

In 1997, about 56,000 people in the United States alone were awaiting organ transplants. According to the United Network for Organ Sharing, about 4,000 died while waiting. This problem is unlikely to be solved unless drastic measures are taken to increase donations. The shortage of organs is such that a few bioethicists have begun to suggest payments to families of the deceased, a measure that has generally been rejected in most nations because it "commodifies" the human body. In parts of Asia, payments have led to an illegal traffic in human organs obtained by questionable means, including organs from living donors. The United States has rejected the concept of implied "state ownership" of bodies after death, followed by mandatory organ donation. Even in countries such as Austria, where cadaver donation appears mandatory unless the deceased has opted out before death, the family's wishes still rule, just as in the United States. Unless most families decide upon donation, it appears that most organs for transplantation will have to come from other sources. Xenotransplantation (use of animal organs that have been specially adapted so as to avoid rejection by the human immune system) is one possibility; this was the original reason for cloning sheep. Xenotransplantation has safety problems, however. Animal infections could cross the "species barrier" into humans.

Growing organs from human embryonic stem cells could avoid the ethical problems inherent in paying or legally coercing families to allow use of the deceased's organs, and could save thousands of lives a year.

Fetal Tissue Research Will Not Increase Abortions

by James Benedict

About the author: *James Benedict is pastor of Union Bridge Church of the Brethren in Union Bridge, Maryland.*

"How dare we kill innocent babies just to make things a little easier for old people?" It was not so much a question as an accusation. Others at the hearing looked expectantly toward me as I stood at the podium. I took a deep breath. Then I tried once again to describe the process by which fetal tissue becomes available for transplantation and its many potential uses for recipients of various ages—including a case in which fetal tissue was transplanted into another fetus in utero.

The asking and answering of that particular question took place four days before delegates to the annual conference of the Church of the Brethren rejected a position paper that expressed cautious and limited approval of fetal tissue use in the treatment of disease or injury. . . .

The question about killing babies to benefit the elderly did more than produce a tense moment. It also reflected two features common to most arguments against fetal tissue use: strong emotion and caricature-like perception of the practice of fetal tissue procurement and transplantation. Current fetal tissue therapy and experimentation programs in the U.S. obtain fetal tissue from legal abortions under strict National Institutes of Health guidelines. These guidelines insist on anonymity between donor and recipient (so one cannot direct that fetal tissue be donated to help a loved one) and forbid payment to the woman who makes tissue available, thus undercutting what might otherwise be strong incentives for abortion.

The guidelines also require that signed consent to abort be obtained before the option of fetal tissue donation is discussed. The goal is to keep separate the decision to abort and the decision to allow the fetal tissue to be used. Indeed, the woman seeking the abortion does not know with certainty that her fetal tissue will be used, thus limiting the significance of general altruism as an incentive to abort.

Fetal tissue obtained under these guidelines is used or may one day be used to treat a wide range of conditions, most notably neural, hematological and endocrine disorders. The condition which has received the most publicity is Parkinson's Syndrome, which commonly manifests itself among older persons. This has led to the charge that fetal tissue use sacrifices the very young in order to benefit those who have already had a long, full life. Other promising uses of fetal tissue, however, include the treatment of conditions hardly restricted to the elderly: diabetes, spinal cord damage and blood diseases.

An Extension of Organ Donation

In many ways, fetal tissue transplantation is merely an extension of organ donation, which has been under way for decades. Instead of replacing whole organs, however, fetal tissue therapy replaces groups of missing or defective cells. Fetal tissue has two advantages over tissue from adults or even newborns. First, fetal cells are relatively undifferentiated and therefore more versatile in their ability to establish residency and function normally in a recipient. Second, fetal cells are less readily recognized as foreign by the recipient's immune system and therefore are less likely to be rejected.

Those who favor using fetal tissue often concede that elective abortion is morally troubling. Some call it a sin, or even "murder." But they argue that this does not preclude the possibility of using the tissue, since organs and tissues for transplant typically come from tragic events, including murder. They claim that agreeing to the use of fetal tissue does not imply approval of past abortions or encouragement of future abortions, any more than the transplantation of a heart or kidney implies approval of—or encourages—drunk driving, domestic violence or drive-by shootings.

Yet as opponents to the use of fetal tissue are quick to point out, the use of tissue from elective abortions differs in at least two important ways from the common practice of using organs and tissues from people who have died. First, organs and tissues for transplantation from the "postborn" tend to become available through events that are either unintended or illegal. The primary source of fetal tissue (elective abortion), on the other hand, is both intentional and legal. Many opponents to fetal tissue use believe that without legal sanctions against elective abortion, the widespread, successful use of fetal tissue to heal will inevitably lead to abortions that would not otherwise have occurred.

> *"The goal is to keep separate the decision to abort and the decision to allow the fetal tissue to be used."*

The second important difference between fetal tissue use and other tissue and organ transplantation concerns the issue of consent. Consent to use hearts, kidneys, corneas and lungs typically comes from the next of kin, who may know the donor's own feelings or expressed wishes about donation. Further, that next of kin would only in rare cases be responsible for the death of the donor. By contrast, consent for the use of fetal tissue is made by the woman who has requested the abortion.

Many who favor fetal tissue use in general see a problem here. Some have suggested establishing bioethics committees to offer or deny consent on a case-by-case basis. Others have called for a policy of presumed con-

> *"The use of fetal tissue does not imply approval of past abortions or encouragement of future abortions."*

sent, under which the tissue may be collected for use unless the woman (or in some cases another family member) objects. Still others have expressed their concern about consent through semantics, insisting that only the fetus itself be called the "donor," or that the tissue be referred to as the woman's "contribution" but not as her "gift."

Because of the legality of abortion and the knotty problems that arise around the matter of consent, it is impossible to regard fetal tissue use as the ethical equivalent of organ and tissue transplantation from postborn donors. But this does not necessarily mean that Christian faith requires us to avoid or forbid participation in fetal tissue experimentation or therapy.

Those who oppose the use of fetal tissue tend to ignore how often scripture and tradition emphasize healing, even in ways that raise moral concerns. According to the Jewish tradition, all but three commandments in the Torah may be violated in order to save a life (idolatry, adultery and murder). Jesus was well within this tradition when he violated purity and Sabbath law in his own ministry of healing.

Scripture and tradition thus challenge arguments against fetal tissue use based on the moral questions surrounding the issue of consent and concerns about appearing to endorse the act of abortion. The obligation to save and heal takes precedence over these.

The Effects

What remains to be considered are the effects that widespread, successful use of fetal tissue may have on the number of subsequent abortions, and the degree to which those who recommend, transplant or accept fetal tissue will be responsible for those effects. As long as the guidelines require anonymity between donor and recipient and prohibit any form of compensation for women whose fetuses are used, general altruism would be the only added incentive for women to seek abortions. Most who have considered the issue, especially women, tend to feel this would lead to few additional abortions, if any. The physical and emotional risks of abortion are simply too great to be significantly influenced by the idea that one's abortion might possibly do a stranger some good.

Still, one cannot deny the possibility that a woman might be moved to abort by the thought that her abortion might do someone some good through fetal tissue transplantation. In this case, the parallel with organ and tissue donation from postborn donors is apt. There is certainly nothing to prevent a would-be murderer from deciding to go ahead on the basis of his knowledge that the intended victim has an organ donor card. Although both scenarios are highly unlikely, neither is completely beyond the realm of imagination. The point is that the act is not justified by the incentive. Those who have retrieved, transplanted or received tissues and organs in the past are not morally responsible for the decision the other person made.

In the biblical description of the entry of suffering and evil into human experience (Gen. 3), it is made clear that suffering and evil become intertwined with the good that God has created. All our efforts to alleviate one particular form of suffering involve the risk of perpetuating or increasing some other form of suffering. This is clearly the case when we consider the unfortunate symbiotic relationship between elective abortion and fetal tissue transplantation.

Some Christians may choose to suffer or die rather than benefit from an act they consider morally reprehensible or risk creating a morally insufficient incentive for any future abortion. Our tradition of respect for individual conscience, grounded in New Testament teaching (e.g., Rom. 14:13ff.), leads us to acknowledge the validity of such a perspective. Patients must always be informed of the intention to use fetal tissue so that those who wish may decline it.

But those who might choose to suffer or even die themselves do not have the right to require others to become unwilling martyrs. In cases where no other treatment of equal or greater effectiveness is available, and the guidelines prohibiting designated donations and payment are followed, persons may recommend, choose and participate in fetal tissue transplantation without violating their covenant with God or the church.

> *"The physical and emotional risks of abortion are simply too great to be significantly influenced by the idea that one's abortion might possibly do a stranger some good."*

We should vigorously pursue the research and development of treatment options that may decrease or replace the use of fetal tissue. We should renew and continue efforts to reduce the number of abortions, without regard for how the reduction might affect the supply of fetal tissue for transplantation. We should hope for and work toward a time in which the use of tissue from elective abortions is replaced by other treatments. But meanwhile we must live with respect and compassion in this time when fetal tissue is the last, best or only hope for some.

Fetal Tissue Transplants Are Ineffective

by Paul Ranalli

About the author: *Paul Ranalli is a neurologist at the University of Toronto and a member of the advisory council of the deVeber Institute for Bioethics and Social Research.*

The hugely unimpressive outcome of a four-year-long clinical trial that injected brain tissue harvested from aborted babies in an attempt to treat Parkinson's disease was well hidden in recent reports in the mainstream media. Indeed, just reading the headlines of the findings, presented in Toronto at the 1999 annual meeting of the American Academy of Neurology, the reader could altogether miss how abysmal were the results of the controversial surgery.

For example, Parkinson's is a disease in which the overwhelming majority of patients are senior citizens. Yet the controversial fetal transplants were found to be ineffective for anyone over 60 years of age. Even among the younger patients in the study, the claimed benefits are limited and qualified.

However, these bottom-line outcomes were well hidden in the rose-tinted press coverage. "Hints of success in fetal cell transplants" (*New York Times*) and "Parkinson's progress" (*Medical Post*) stretched the minimally positive results to the breaking point. The *Washington Post*'s statement "Fetal cell implants may benefit younger Parkinson's patients" was at least slightly more realistic.

In fact the supposed benefits were extremely marginal. Were the claims of proponents treated less uncritically, these fetal tissue results could represent the beginning of the end of this unethical chapter in neurological research. Unfortunately, the message may take some time to reach the public, given years of unjustified hype and falsely elevated expectations.

The First Time Vigorously Tested

The results were announced in April 1999, 11 years after President Ronald Reagan first banned taxpayer support of fetal tissue transplants from aborted babies and six years after Bill Clinton lifted the ban. The long-awaited study

Reprinted from Paul Ranalli, "Media Sugarcoats Fetal Tissue Transplant Failure," *National Right to Life News*, June 10, 1999. Reprinted with permission from the author.

funded to the tune of $5.7 million by the National Institute of Neurological Disorders and Stroke (NINDS) was the first time the much-hyped fetal tissue transplant experiments were subjected to what scientists call "placebo control." Previously, reports of patient benefits lacked a control group against which to measure alleged improvements.

The four-year study was led by Dr. Curt Freed of the University of Colorado in Denver and Dr. Stanley Fahn of Columbia Presbyterian Center in Manhattan. It was highly controversial, not only because of the use of tissue from aborted babies, but also because only half of the patients received the fetal brain tissue.

Once chosen for the study, the 40 patients with advanced Parkinson's disease were assigned randomly to either of two groups. For the "treatment group," the team of doctors from New York and Colorado implanted brain tissue from four aborted fetuses deep in the patients' brains.

A second group (the "placebo" group) underwent a "sham" operation, in which holes were drilled in their skulls. Going in, each patient knew he or she had only a 50–50 chance of actually receiving a fetal tissue implant.

The Placebo Effect

Once the patient's scalp was sewn up and the head bandage applied, there was no outward difference in the appearance of the two groups, ensuring an equal distribution of the "placebo effect." (By this scientists mean the powerful positive benefit on the mind and motivation of a patient who has the belief that an effective treatment has been applied.)

As it turns out, a number of patients from both the placebo group (sham surgery) and the group that received a fetal tissue transplant felt remarkably better after the operation. Dr. Fahn told the *New York Times*, "They got this placebo surgery and immediately they felt better." He noted that the feeling of well-being lasted throughout the year of follow-up.

In addition to self-assessment scores in which patients rated how they were doing, a series of thorough examinations were carried out by a team of neurologists who, like the patients, were "blinded" from knowing whether the patient actually received fetal tissue.

> *"For the group with the worst cases of Parkinson's, fetal tissue transplantation is a complete failure."*

Patients were followed for one year, after which the blinding was broken and they were informed whether they had actually received fetal tissue or a sham procedure.

At that point the placebo patients were offered the opportunity to have the fetal transplant at a second operation. Fourteen of the 20 patients who underwent the sham surgery elected to have the surgery.

According to the *New York Times,* a second team, led by Dr. C. Warren Olanow of the Mt. Sinai School of Medicine in New York, has also received a grant. This group's results will be reported on in 2001.

Parkinson's disease is generally thought to be caused by the death of cells that make dopamine, a chemical that transmits messages in the brain. It is a slowly degenerative disorder characterized by body tremor, slowness of movement, muscle rigidity, and loss of balance, with onset generally between age 50 and 70, with a peak onset in the early 60s.

> *"When one looks at the scant data presented, . . . a magnifying glass is required to discern any functional benefit."*

For patients over 60, no difference was observed in the tests between the placebo group and the group who received fetal tissue, either on the neurologists' examinations or the patients' own perception of how they were doing. In other words, for the group with the worse cases of Parkinson's, fetal tissue transplantation is a complete failure.

Although there is yet no cure for the disease, which affects an estimated one million Americans, symptoms are initially mild, and can be well treated by a variety of medications, especially for the first five years. Eventually, symptoms progress, requiring larger doses of drugs, which are eventually used in combination. Ultimately, the drugs begin to lose their efficacy, and the larger doses required cause unwanted side effects.

It is at this stage that surgical treatments have recently been considered. Aside from the unproven fetal transplants, there are in fact other ethically sound surgical procedures (pallidotomy, deep brain stimulation) which have high success rates, demonstrated in a number of published reports.

A small number of Parkinson's disease patients, like actor Michael J. Fox, first develop symptoms at a much younger age. Mercifully, only an estimated 10% of patients present with symptoms below age 50, half of which (5%) begin below age 40. It usually takes 12–14 years before a patient declines to the stage where drugs afford only limited benefit.

In the NINDS fetal transplant trial, participants had suffered from Parkinson's disease for an average 13.4 years. Thus it is likely that no more than 5% of patients (one in 20) might ever progress to the stage where surgery would be considered below age 60.

"Success"?

And what of the touted "success" of this trial in patients under 60 years of age? When one looks at the scant data presented, which has still not been subjected to peer-reviewed publication, a magnifying glass is required to discern any functional benefit.

Improvement was noted only in bradykinesia (slowness of movement) and rigidity (stiffness of muscles). Consider the following results in the younger group for whom the fetal transplants are reported to have "worked":

• No change in "freezing," a sudden, disturbing loss of all movement.

- No improvement in initiating walking.
- No improvement in tremor, one of the hallmark signs of Parkinson's disease.
- No improvement in walking balance.
- No lessening in the number of falls.
- No improvement in dyskinesias, the troubling extra body movements that appear in advanced patients.

And this was for the younger group of patients, the group reported as showing benefit. However, even among the younger patients, individual outcomes were unpredictable. "There's enormous individual variation," stated Dr. Gerald Fischbach, director of the NINDS (which funded the study), to the *Washington Post*. "This is not a yes or no thing."

Also putting a brave face on the results was Dr. Curt Freed of Colorado, co-director of the study with Dr. Fahn. "We need to reduce the variability of the transplant response," Dr. Freed told the *New York Times*. Others were more direct. Dr. J. William Langston, president of the Parkinson's Institute, told the *Times*, "I'm disappointed the results were not more dramatic."

Two patients who received the fetal transplants later died from causes stated to be unrelated to the implant surgery. Autopsies of their brains showed survival and growth of the transplanted fetal cells, at seven months and three years after surgery, respectively.

Proponents of the study used these results to claim the transplant concept is a viable one. However, it turns out that the presence of strong regrowth did not correlate with improvement in function.

> *"Fetal transplantation in Parkinson's disease has been found sorely lacking, even among those for whom there is no ethical dilemma."*

Patients in the study were given PET brain scans, which can indicate how much of the depleted brain chemical dopamine is being secreted in various parts of the brain. Two-thirds of patients had at least a 20% improvement in dopamine signal from the transplanted area, in both the older and younger groups. Yet the older patients showed no functional improvement at all.

This led Long Island's Dr. David Eidelberg, who performed the scans, to ask rhetorically, "So why didn't the older group show the improvement the younger group did?"

Alternatives to Fetal Tissue Transplants

Fortunately for patients with Parkinson's disease, the present and future looks promising along other therapeutic avenues. The sources come either from non-human sources or from within the patient's own brain.

A multi-center human trial utilizing brain tissue from embryonic pigs is underway. Just recently, a startling result was announced from Spain, where researchers working with monkeys extracted cells from a site near the carotid artery in the neck and transplanted them into the monkeys' own brains, where they produced the key neuro-chemical dopamine at 35 times the rate of fetal cells. This raises the possibility of a Parkinson's patient being able to be his own donor, utilizing a group of cells with potentially far greater efficacy.

The emerging field of stem cell research (involving stems cells from sources other than human embryos) also looks exciting. Stem cells are developmentally "young," capable of "differentiating" into a number of specialized body cells, such as bone, muscle, and brain cells. While early research found these cells in embryos, new evidence reveals they may lurk in various regions of adult humans.

Parkinson's disease expert Dr. Mark Guttman of the University of Toronto points out that up to 3% of brain cells in a person's gray matter may actually be a form of neural-based stem cell. A pool of these cells can be extracted from brain tissue removed from humans for a variety of therapeutic reasons, then cultured, stored, and eventually encouraged to mature into dopamine-producing cells, suitable for transplant.

Finally subject to the stringent placebo-controlled standards of the rest of medical research, fetal transplantation in Parkinson's disease has been found sorely lacking, even among those for whom there is no ethical dilemma. The research world has largely moved on, turning the page on yet another attempt by abortion advocates to fashion an altruistic spin on modern medicine's most shameful ongoing practice.

Fetal Tissue Transplants Are Immoral

by Center for Biblical Bioethics

About the author: *The Center for Biblical Bioethics, a division of Baptists for Life, uses biblical principles to evaluate moral issues in the biotechnology and medical fields.*

When a Baptist minister spoke to Congress in favor of government funding of fetal tissue transplants, he claimed to represent a pro-life point of view. Sprinkling his presentation with quotes from the Bible, he told a congressional subcommittee that it was "pro-life" to support any treatment that saves lives. He asserted that God approved of tissue transplants in general because He performed the first one, referring to the creation of Eve.

The minister was motivated to advocate transplants from aborted babies because his youngest child benefited from a fetal-to-fetal bone marrow transplant to correct a congenital deficiency that killed two of his other four children. His son did not benefit from an abortion, however, but received live fetal stem cells from an ectopic pregnancy. It remains to be seen whether the operation was successful.

Advocates of fetal tissue transplants argue that ectopic pregnancies and spontaneous miscarriages are too unpredictable and will not yield enough tissue for all the potential uses. Tissue must be fresh, disease free, and at the right age for it to grow and proliferate in its new site. The remains of aborted babies are needed, they say, to meet the demand.

Fetal tissue transplants are proposed as a treatment for a wide variety of heartbreaking ailments: Alzheimer's, Huntington's and Parkinson's diseases, epilepsy, spinal injuries, stroke, diabetes, and hemophilia, as well as birth defects. It is estimated that 10 million Americans could be helped by the surgical injection of fetal tissue into affected areas. Researchers say that fetal tissue is not rejected like other transplants, and that it multiplies and flourishes, differentiates and synthesizes while tissue from adults does not. In theory, fetal tissue

Excerpted from "What About Fetal Tissue Transplants?" an online article from the Center for Biblical Bioethics at www.bfl.org/cbb/fetal.html. Reprinted with permission from the Center for Biblical Bioethics.

stimulates the growth of healthy cells, which in turn restores health to the affected individual.

The Pro-Life Response

In opposing the destruction of unborn human life, the pro-life movement rejects the use of electively aborted tissues for any purpose. Treating tissues this way further diminishes the value of the unborn child, who becomes little more than an assemblage of spare parts.

Fetal tissue transplantation also legitimates abortion in the minds of those who procure and perform them. Already, women have offered to become pregnant in order to provide compatible fetal tissue for loved ones.

Pro-lifers point out the bizarre twist of logic advocates of fetal tissue transplants make in denying the humanity of the unborn child while insisting such procedures work because the donors are human. Drs. Paul O'Connor and Paul Ranalli, of the division of Neurology at the University of Toronto, describe the dilemma this way: "One simply cannot have it both ways. The first-trimester fetus cannot be simultaneously both a 'blob' and a human being with a specialized brain structure suitable for transplant. And after eight weeks, the fetal brain only becomes more mature, more developed, more specialized."

Finally, pro-lifers believe that no matter how promising the use of fetal tissue is in alleviating the suffering of others, no sufferer should expect another to die that he or she might live. One woman diagnosed with Parkinson's disease courageously declared, "I have made up my mind that I will refuse any prescription or treatment that involves using fetal tissue. My life is no more valuable than that of the baby who would be giving its life—not for my life, but for my comfort."

How Is Fetal Tissue Obtained?

Dr. Bernard Nathanson has explained the gruesome procedure by which brain cells are obtained from unborn babies: "Pregnant women at 13–18 weeks are placed on an operating table, the cervix is dilated, the bag of water is broken, the fetal head is guided into position just above the open cervix, the fetal skull is then drilled open and a suction device is placed into the brain. The brain substance is then suctioned out and placed immediately on ice to preserve its viability, then the fetus is aborted, i.e. destroyed in the abortion

> *"The unborn child . . . becomes little more than an assemblage of spare parts."*

process. Similar procedures are used to harvest fetal pancreas, fetal liquid and fetal thymus." This alone should discourage anyone from supporting fetal tissue transplants.

Clearly, the act of retrieving tissue from unborn babies is what kills them, not a separate, prior event such as a suction abortion. Furthermore, medical technicians are sometimes stationed in abortion clinics to sort out the good fetal remains from the bad. The nation's largest supplier of fetal tissue, the International Institute for the Advancement of Medicine, advertises for doctors who use particular abortion methods so they can obtain intact tissue. Tissue obtained through saline abortions is no good since the babies will have been dead too long. Similarly, very early abortions—those caused by RU-486, for instance—will yield tissue too young for use.

Such a procedure also endangers women. It is done later in pregnancy and takes longer than normal abortion procedures. Janice Raymond, a professor at MIT and the University of Massachusetts and an advocate of abortion "rights," worries that fetal tissue transplants will greatly increase the number of abortions and turn women into factories for spare parts.

How Successful Have Fetal Transplants Been?

A December 1994 announcement led many to believe fetal tissue transplants done by a team of scientists at Dalhousie University in Halifax, Nova Scotia, had proven resoundingly successful. But Dr. Ranalli, writing in the January 1995 issue of *National Right to Life News* revealed that after the initial report, no data from the Halifax study had been published. He quoted lead Halifax researcher Dr. Alan Fine as saying, "We have an intriguing and perhaps disturbing suggestion that the progression of the disease may continue after [an] initial graft-associated improvement. . . . Eventually disease progression continues . . . and patient performance starts to deteriorate."

> *"Clearly, the act of retrieving tissue from unborn babies is what kills them, not a separate, prior event such as a suction abortion."*

A *British Medical Journal* review stated that "So far probably more patients have been harmed than have been helped." Concerns are raised over the potential for spreading HIV and other diseases through fetal tissue transplants.

Dr. Nathanson's assessment of fetal tissue transplants is the most brutal:

> When one peruses the available medical literature critically and sets aside optimistic prediction and pseudoscientific boosterism, the results have been—in a word—lousy. Transplantation of fetal pancreatic cells (so-called 'islet cells') to adult diabetics has been attempted in more than 100 cases with no successes: in every case the graft has died and the diabetes has been unrelieved. . . . In not one single case [of transplant for treatment of Parkinson's and other diseases] has there been anything approaching a cure or even a permanent remission. In short, the clinical experience in treating adult disease with fetal tissue transplants has been expensive, uniformly disappointing and unpromising.

Failure is not surprising when one considers the many obstacles to successful fetal tissue transplantation. Dr. Ranalli points out that "the tiny dopamine-secreting cells must be identified and collected from the dismembered fetal brain; they must survive the suction forces of the vacuum extraction and the subsequent handling; they must survive a period of time in preservatives; they must survive injection through a syringe, implantation deep inside a foreign brain, the trauma and hemorrhage of the needle stab, the inevitable confrontation with the host's immune system, and, finally, establish enduring and accurate links with the appropriate cells in the relevant parts of the recipient brain, while the brain's defenses try to wall off the invading cells with scar tissue and killer immune cells."

> *"The clinical experience in treating adult disease with fetal tissue transplants has been . . . uniformly disappointing and unpromising."*

Why, then, is the medical community's eagerness for fetal tissue transplantation unabated? William M. Landau, M.D., a prominent neurologist, says, "This is not just an issue of bent statistics; rather it is one of lost scientific principles. There is simply no evidence to prove that either clinical or experimental parkinsonism in primates is specifically cured by transplantation of tissue into the brain."

Advocates of fetal tissue transplants from aborted babies accuse opponents of hypocrisy. They say that most Americans, including pro-lifers, have already benefited from tissues obtained from aborted babies by having polio vaccines. Vaccine cultures were supposedly cultivated in cells from aborted babies. This claim is erroneous, however. Dr. Peter McCullagh, the Senior Fellow in Developmental Physiology at the John Curtin School of Medical Research at Australian National University, says that "by the time that production of polio virus to be tested as a vaccine in human subjects commenced, cells from monkey kidneys had become the preferred source of tissue." He cited many possible sources for the tissues and went on to say that "the entirety of world production of polio vaccine between 1968 and the late 1970s appears to have been achieved with the progeny of one fetal cell line. . . . Attempts to assert that polio vaccine could not have been developed if fetal tissue had not been used represent selective amnesia."

Are There Alternatives?

Alternatives to fetal tissue transplants include the following:
- Cell lines derived from miscarriages or ectopic pregnancies. This source of tissue has been proposed in Congress, although an argument can be made against using ectopic embryos this way.
- The drug THA, or Cognex for Alzheimer's patients. So far, the Food and Drug Administration has refused to approve its use in the United States.
- Gene therapy for Parkinson's sufferers. Although controversial, the technique, which slips an enzyme into the patient's skin cells, "stimulates cells to make and secrete dopamine."
- Stem cell stimulation. Until recently, it was thought that we had our full

complement of brain cells at birth. Fetal cells supposedly stimulate brain cell growth, but scientists have found that some embryonic stem cells survive dormant in the adult brain and can be stimulated to enable the brain to repair itself.

- Gm1 ganglioside. Found in the membranes of many nerve cells and derived from any mammal, such as a cow, this substance also stimulates damaged brain cells to repair themselves. This treatment has already been beneficial for people with spinal cord injuries.
- Pallidotomy. Microscopic surgical lesions in the pallidum structure of the brain improve muscle function in Parkinson's patients.
- Brain pacemaker. Tiny devices placed in the brain offer chronic stimulation.

What Guidance Do We Have from Scripture?

Of course, the Bible does not mention fetal tissue transplants, but it is clear we should have respect for human life. In Genesis 4:10–11, God Himself avenges the murder of innocent people. He hates hands that shed innocent blood (Proverbs 6:17). He has no pleasure in sacrifices offered by bloody hands (Isaiah 1:11,15).

One passage, Exodus 21:28, prevents people from directly benefiting from the death of a human being: "If an ox gore a man or a woman, that they die: then the ox shall be surely stoned, and his flesh shall not be eaten."

An ox was a valuable commodity in Israel's economy—good for labor, food, and sacrificial giving. But in God's economy, the ox that killed someone was put to death immediately, preventing further service in the field. It was killed by stoning, preventing its use as a sacrifice to God, as good a motive as that might be. Its carcass was not to be eaten, even by the bereaved family. In a strictly temporal sense, the ox was wasted.

Many arguments could be made against wasting such an ox. In years of famine, an ox roast would feed many hungry people. Why not at least reap some spiritual benefits by offering the beast in sacrifice? Why kill it at all, since by dying it would not bring back the dead person?

These arguments are echoed in the current debate over fetal tissue transplants: "Why not use the bodies of aborted babies for doing good? Destined for the incinerator, their bodies might as well benefit the living."

David understood and lived out the sanctity of human life principle. When three of his mighty men risked their lives to bring him water from the well of Bethlehem, he "wasted" it (II Samuel 23:15–17). He poured it out on the ground even though he was thirsty, saying, "Be it far from me, O Lord, that I should do this: is not this the blood of the men that went in jeopardy of their lives?" It is safe to say that, were David living today, he would not accept a tissue transplant from an aborted baby.

Thus, one human life is not to be placed over against another. No one individual is more valuable than another; both are infinitely valuable. A benefit to a living person should not be used as moral justification for killing someone else.

Bibliography

Books

Dallas A. Blanchard	*The Anti-Abortion Movement: References and Resources.* New York: G.K. Hall, 1996.
James F. Bohan	*The House of Atreus: Abortion as a Human Rights Issue.* Westport, CT: Praeger, 1999.
Mary Boyle	*Re-thinking Abortion: Psychology, Gender, Power, and the Law.* New York: Routledge, 1997.
Geoffrey G. Drutchas	*Is Life Sacred?* Cleveland: Pilgrim, 1998.
Susan Dwyer and Joel Feinberg, eds.	*The Problem of Abortion.* 3rd ed. Belmont, CA: Wadsworth, 1997.
Keith A. Fournier and William D. Watkins	*In Defense of Life.* Colorado Springs: NavPress, 1996.
David J. Garrow	*Liberty and Sexuality: The Right to Privacy and the Making of "Roe v. Wade."* Berkeley: University of California Press, 1998.
Cynthia Gorney	*Articles of Faith: A Frontline History of the Abortion Wars.* New York: Simon and Schuster, 1998.
Mark A. Graber	*Rethinking Abortion: Equal Choice, the Constitution, and Reproductive Politics.* Princeton, NJ: Princeton University Press, 1996.
Mary Guiden	*Partial Birth Abortion.* Denver: National Conference of State Legislatures, 1998.
Janet Hadley	*Abortion: Between Freedom and Necessity.* Philadelphia: Temple University Press, 1996.
Cecil Kirk Hutson	*"Dilation and Extraction" Abortions: Medical Procedure or Infanticide?* Sacramento, CA: Assembly Publications Office, 1996.
Kerry N. Jacoby	*Souls, Bodies, Spirits: The Drive to Abolish Abortion Since 1973.* Westport, CT: Praeger, 1998.
Angela Kennedy, ed.	*Swimming Against the Tide: Feminist Dissent on the Issue of Abortion.* Dublin, Ireland: Open Air, 1997.

Peter Korn   *Lovejoy: A Year in the Life of an Abortion Clinic.* 1st ed. New York: Atlantic Monthly, 1996.

Alison Landes et al., eds.   *Abortion: An Eternal Social and Moral Issue.* Wylie, TX: Information Plus, 1996.

Ellie Lee, ed.   *Abortion Law and Politics Today.* New York: St. Martin's, 1998.

Patrick Lee   *Abortion and Unborn Human Life.* Washington, DC: Catholic University of America Press, 1996.

Eileen L. McDonagh   *Breaking the Abortion Deadlock: From Choice to Consent.* New York: Oxford University Press, 1996.

Bernard N. Nathanson   *The Hand of God: A Journey from Death to Life by the Abortion Doctor Who Changed His Mind.* Washington, DC: Regnery, 1996.

Louis P. Pojman and Francis J. Beckwith, eds.   *The Abortion Controversy: Twenty-Five Years After "Roe v. Wade": A Reader.* 2nd ed. Belmont, CA: Wadsworth, 1998.

Suzanne T. Poppema and Mike Henderson   *Why I Am an Abortion Doctor.* Amherst, NY: Prometheus Books, 1996.

Andrea Lee Press and Elizabeth R. Cole   *Speaking of Abortion: Television and Authority in the Lives of Women.* Chicago: University of Chicago Press, 1999.

R. Randall Rainey and Gerard Magill, eds.   *Abortion and Public Policy: An Interdisciplinary Investigation Within the Catholic Tradition.* Omaha: Creighton University Press, 1996.

Jeffrey H. Reiman   *Abortion and the Ways We Value Human Life.* Lanham, MD: Rowman and Littlefield, 1999.

Kathy Rudy   *Beyond Pro-Life and Pro-Choice: Moral Diversity in the Abortion Debate.* Boston: Beacon, 1996.

Rickie Solinger, ed.   *Abortion Wars: A Half Century of Struggle, 1950–2000.* Berkeley: University of California Press, 1998.

Lloyd Steffen, ed.   *Abortion: A Reader.* Cleveland: Pilgrim, 1996.

Brad Stetson, ed.   *The Silent Subject: Reflections on the Unborn in American Culture.* Westport, CT: Praeger, 1996.

Raymond Tatalovich   *The Politics of Abortion in the United States and Canada: A Comparative Study.* Armonk, NY: M.E. Sharpe, 1997.

Kevin William Wildes and Alan C. Mitchell, eds.   *Choosing Life: A Dialogue on "Evangelium Vitae."* Washington, DC: Georgetown University Press, 1997.

Periodicals

George J. Annas   "Partial-Birth Abortion, Congress, and the Constitution," *New England Journal of Medicine,* July 23, 1998. Available from 10 Shattuck St., Boston, MA 02115-6094.

Bibliography

James Benedict   "The Use of Fetal Tissue," *Christian Century*, February 18, 1998.

Gillian Bentley   "Doing What Comes Naturally," *New Scientist*, August 31, 1996.

Angela Bonavoglia   "Separating Fact from Fiction," *Ms.*, May/June 1997.

James Bopp and Curtis R. Cook   "Partial-Birth Abortion: The Final Frontier of Abortion Jurisprudence," *Issues in Law & Medicine*, Summer 1998.

Elinor Burkett   "The Last Abortion: How Science Could Silence the Debate," *Utne Reader*, May/June 1998.

Sidney Callahan   "Bad Arguments: Twenty-Five Years After 'Roe,'" *Commonweal*, January 30, 1998.

Brae Canlen   "The Long Labor of RU 486: Politics, Protests, and Litigation Have Delayed the Controversial Abortion Pill," *California Lawyer*, May 1997.

Joanne Chen   "The Aftermath of *Roe v. Wade*," *Vogue*, January 1998.

Sally B. Donnelly   "The Real Partial-Birth War," *Time*, October 20, 1997.

Cynthia Gorney   "Caught in the Crossfire: Will the War on Reproductive Rights Ever End?" *Utne Reader*, May/June 1998.

David A. Grimes   "Continuing Need for Late Abortions," *JAMA*, August 26, 1998. Available from PO Box 10946, Chicago, IL 60610.

Jo Ann Harris, Deval Patrick, and Susan Finn   "Is the Federal Law Making It a Crime to Block Abortion Clinics Fair to Anti-Abortion Protestors?" *CQ Researcher*, April 7, 1995. Available from 1414 22nd St. NW, Washington, DC 20037.

William Harrison   "Abortion: One Doctor's Story," *Vogue*, January 1998.

Jack Hitt   "Who Will Do Abortions Here?" *New York Times Magazine*, January 19, 1998.

Jennifer Hunter   "A Dangerous Time of Year: The Killing of a U.S. Doctor Heightens Fears Among Abortionists," *Maclean's*, November 2, 1998.

Marianne Lavelle   "When Abortions Come Late in a Pregnancy," *U.S. News & World Report*, January 19, 1998.

Tamar Lewin   "Debate Distant for Many Having Abortions," *New York Times*, January 17, 1998.

Tamar Lewin   "Study on a Late Term Abortion Finds Procedure Is Little Used," *New York Times*, December 11, 1998.

Maggie O'Shaughnessy   "The Worst of Both Worlds? Parental Involvement Requirements and the Privacy Rights of Mature Minors," *Ohio State Law Journal*, November 1996.

Edith L. Pacillo   "Expanding the Feminist Imagination: An Analysis of Reproductive Rights," *American University Journal of Gender & the Law*, Fall 1997.

The Abortion Controversy

Katha Pollitt — "Murder Inc.," *Nation,* November 16, 1998.

Katha Pollitt — "*Roe v. Wade* at Twenty-Five," *Nation,* February 2–9, 1998.

Progressive — "The Preachers of Hate," December 1998.

Hanna Rosin — "Outside Laboratory, Moral Objections: Abortion Foes Oppose Embryo Research," *Washington Post,* November 6, 1998.

Wendy Shalit — "Whose Choice? Abortion Is Supposed to Empower Women. Tell That to a Girl in Trouble," *National Review,* May 18, 1998.

Deborah L. Shelton — "Abortion Alternative: There's a Safe New Choice for Women Facing Unwanted Pregnancies," *Essence,* January 1997.

Amanda Swarr — "Terrorism and Murder: The True Intent of the 'Pro-Life' Movement Exposed," *Off Our Backs,* May 1995.

Meredith Wadman — "Embryo Research Is Pro-Life," *New York Times,* February 21, 1996.

Betsy Wagner — "Who Has Abortions?" *U.S. News & World Report,* August 19, 1996.

Steven Waldman, Elise Ackerman, and Rita Rubin — "Hard Choices," *U.S. News & World Report*, January 19, 1998.

Robert J. White — "Partial-Birth Abortion: A Neurosurgeon Speaks," *America,* October 18, 1997.

Michael Sean Winters — "Stand by Them! A New Strategy for the Pro-Life Movement," *America,* April 19, 1997.

Organizations to Contact

The editors have compiled the following list of organizations concerned with the issues presented in this book. The descriptions are derived from materials provided by the organizations. All have publications or information available for interested readers. The list was compiled on the date of publication of the present volume; the information provided here may change. Be aware that many organizations take several weeks or longer to respond to inquiries, so allow as much time as possible.

Alan Guttmacher Institute (AGI)
120 Wall St., New York, NY 10005
(212) 248-1111 • fax: (212) 248-1951
e-mail: info@agi-usa.org • website: www.agi-usa.org

AGI works to safeguard the reproductive rights of women and men worldwide. The institute advocates the right to a safe and legal abortion and provides extensive statistical information on abortion. Its publications include the policy papers "Teenagers' Right to Consent to Reproductive Health Care" and "Late-Term Abortions: Legal Considerations."

American Life League (ALL)
PO Box 1350, Stafford, VA 22535
(540) 659-4171
website: www.all.org

ALL is a Christian organization whose goal is to protect human life—from fertilization to natural death—and to encourage respect of its sanctity. The league opposes abortion and stem cell research, and it publishes related articles in its *Celebrate Life* magazine, published six times a year.

Catholics for a Free Choice (CFFC)
1436 U St. NW, Suite 301, Washington, DC 20009-3997
(202) 986-6093 • fax: (202) 332-7995
e-mail: cffc@catholicsforchoice.org • website: www.catholicsforchoice.org

Catholics for a Free Choice supports the right to a legal abortion. It promotes family planning to reduce the incidence of abortion and to increase women's choices in childbearing and child rearing. CFFC's website lists full-text electronic articles such as "The Roman Catholic Church and Reproductive Choice" as well as summaries of pro-choice Catholic books. In addition, it publishes the quarterly *Conscience* magazine.

Center for Bioethics and Human Dignity (CBHD)
2065 Half Day Rd., Bannockburn, Il 60015
(847) 317-8180 • fax: (847) 317-8153
e-mail: cbhd@cbhd.org • website: www.bioethix.org

CBHD is an international educational center that examines bioethical issues from a Christian perspective. The center opposes abortion and genetic technologies such as fetal tissue research. It publishes topical articles, public testimonies, and the twice year-ly newsletter *Dignity*.

Feminist Majority Foundation (FMF)

1600 Wilson Blvd., Suite 801, Arlington, VA 22209
(403) 522-2214 • fax: (703) 522-2219
e-mail: femmaj@feminist.org • website: www.feminist.org

FMF advocates political, economic, and social equality for women. The foundation also strives to protect the abortion right for women. It hosts the National Clinic Defense Project and the Campaign for RU-486 and Contraceptive Research. FMF reports on feminist issues, including abortion, in its quarterly *Feminist Majority Report*.

Feminists for Life of America (FFLA)

733 15th St. NW, Suite 1100, Washington, DC 20005
(202) 737-3352
e-mail: fems4life@aol.com • website: www.feministsforlife.org

FFLA is a grassroots, nonsectarian organization that works to achieve equality for women. It opposes abortion and infanticide, considering these acts to be inconsistent with the feminist principles of justice, nonviolence, and nondiscrimination. It publishes the quarterly journal the *American Feminist*, which includes such articles as "The After-math of Abortion."

Human Life International (HLI)

4 Family Life Ln., Front Royal, VA 22630
(540) 635-7884 • fax: (540) 636-7363
e-mail: hli@hli.org • website: www.hli.org

HLI promotes and defends the sanctity of life and family according to the tenets of the Roman Catholic Church. It believes that the fetus is human from the moment of con-ception. Its publications include the monthly newsletter *HLI Reports* and the position papers "Abortion" and "Planned Parenthood."

National Abortion and Reproductive Rights Action League (NARAL)

1156 15th St. NW, Suite 700, Washington, DC 20005
website: www.naral.org

Since 1969, NARAL's mission has been to secure and protect a woman's right to safe, legal abortion. In addition to raising awareness about reproductive rights and lobbying for pro-choice legislation, the league also works to stop antiabortion violence, ensure access to abortion, and combat unplanned pregnancy. NARAL publications include the quarterly *NARAL News* and the book *Choices: Women Speak Out About Abortion*.

National Coalition of Abortion Providers (NCAP)

206 King St., Alexandria, VA 22314
(703) 684-0055 • fax: (703) 684-5051
e-mail: ronncap@aol.com • website: www.ncap.com

NCAP is a pro-choice organization that represents the political interests of independent abortion providers nationwide. The coalition lobbies in Washington, D.C., for pro-choice, pro-provider policies. NCAP publishes the bimonthly newsletter *NCAP News*.

National Right to Life Committee (NRLC)

419 Seventh St. NW, Suite 500, Washington, DC 20004
(202) 626-8800
e-mail: nrlc@nrlc.org • website: www.nrlc.org

NRLC is a pro-life organization that believes that life begins at conception. It considers abortion to be society's greatest injustice. The committee campaigns against legislation to legalize abortion. It encourages ratification of a constitutional amendment granting embryos and fetuses the same right to life as living persons, and it advocates alternatives to abortion, such as adoption. NRLC publications include the monthly *NRL News* and the brochure *When Does Life Begin?*

Planned Parenthood Federation of America (PPFA)
810 Seventh Ave., New York, NY 10019
(212) 541-7800 • fax: (212) 245-1845
e-mail: communications@ppfa.org • website: www.plannedparenthood.org

Planned Parenthood is the world's oldest and largest voluntary family planning organization. The federation works to ensure that all women have legal access to safe abortion and reproductive health care services. PPFA advocates public policies that guarantee reproductive rights, including those of teenagers, and it supports government funding for abortions. The federation publishes the quarterly newsletter *Speak Out!* and articles such as "Mifepristone: The New Face of Abortion."

Pro-Life Action League (PLAL)
6160 N. Cicero Ave., Suite 600, Chicago, IL 60646
(773) 777-2900 • fax: (773) 777-3061
e-mail: scheidler@ibm.net • website: www.prolifeaction.org

PLAL is a pro-life organization dedicated to ending abortion. Working through nonviolent direct action—particularly sidewalk counseling—the league actively protests abortion. Its website contains press releases related to PLAL's current campaigns and its efforts to maintain protesters' access to abortion clinics. Its student research section includes the articles "Back Alley Abortions" and "Sidewalk Counseling."

Religious Coalition for Reproductive Choice (RCRC)
1025 Vermont Ave. NW, Suite 1130, Washington, DC 20005
(202) 628-7700 • fax: (202) 628-7716
e-mail: info@rcrc.org • website: www.rcrc.org

Established in 1973 by both clergy and laity, RCRC is America's only national interfaith pro-choice organization. The organization supports abortion rights, opposes antiabortion violence, and educates policymakers and the public about the diversity of religious perspectives on abortion. Among the coalition's publications are the *Speak Out!* series articles "Most Religious Americans Are Pro-Choice" and "Barriers to Abortion Are Barriers to Justice for Women."

Index

Index

Index